# Lecture Notes in Computer Science     13123

More information about this subseries at https://link.springer.com/bookseries/7412

Jianning Li · Jan Egger (Eds.)

# Towards the Automatization of Cranial Implant Design in Cranioplasty II

Second Challenge, AutoImplant 2021
Held in Conjunction with MICCAI 2021
Strasbourg, France, October 1, 2021
Proceedings

*Editors*
Jianning Li ⓘ
Graz University of Technology
Graz, Austria

University Hospital Essen
Essen, Germany

Jan Egger ⓘ
Graz University of Technology
Graz, Austria

University Hospital Essen
Essen, Germany

ISSN 0302-9743       ISSN 1611-3349 (electronic)
Lecture Notes in Computer Science
ISBN 978-3-030-92651-9      ISBN 978-3-030-92652-6 (eBook)
https://doi.org/10.1007/978-3-030-92652-6

LNCS Sublibrary: SL6 – Image Processing, Computer Vision, Pattern Recognition, and Graphics

This Springer imprint is published by the registered company Springer Nature Switzerland AG
The registered company address is: Gewerbestrasse 11, 6330 Cham, Switzerland

# Preface

Different countries can have difference clinical practices of cranioplasty - a surgical procedure to repair cranial defects. For some countries and clinical institutes, a cranial implant is the primary choice for the repairment of cranial defects. However, the design and manufacturing of cranial implants, especially patient-specific implants (PSIs), remains time-consuming and expensive. Hence, current workflows of cranioplasty demand improvements.

The second AutoImplant cranial implant design challenge (AutoImplant 2021, https://autoimplant2021.grand-challenge.org/) was organized as a satellite event of the Medical Image Computing and Computer Assisted Interventions (MICCAI 2021) conference, focusing specifically on the clinical usability of the automatic cranial implant design algorithms. Thus, three task tracks were created for AutoImplant 2021; Task 1 and Task 3 focused on the generalization ability of the algorithms on varied synthetic defect patterns, as we observed from the prior edition of the challenge that improving the generalization ability is non-trivial, yet essential for the problem of automatic cranial implant design. Task 2 provided 11 pre-cranioplasty skulls with real defects from the clinical routine for a clinical evaluation of the algorithms. Clinical experts were invited to manually assess the clinical usability of the predictions for Task 2 based on a scoring system ranging from 1 point (not usable) to 5 points (flawless). The conference was held virtually on October 1, 2021, and featured 11 talks, including two invited talks from German and American neurosurgeons who specialize in cranioplasty and cranial implant design.

The challenge proceedings are comprised of 10 papers (8–18 pages long), including one invited paper from clinical experts about cranioplasty management. A descriptor for the creation of the Task 1 dataset was also provided by the organizing team members. Clinical experts' evaluations for the Task 2 submissions were compiled as an independent paper, as we believe the qualitative evaluation criteria used by clinical experts are valuable to the (automatic) cranial implant design community since general quantitative metrics alone are not closely correlative of the actual practical usability of the cranial implants. The challenge papers were reviewed in a single-blind manner and each challenge paper received three to four reviews. It was required that, for the camera-ready version of the accepted papers, the reviewers' comments must be addressed and incorporated. There is one paper that got accepted after a major revision.

We are grateful to the organizing team members, the authors, and the speakers for making our conference a success, and for contributing to the advancement of automatic cranial implant design.

October 2021

Jianning Li
Jan Egger

# Organization

## General Chairs

Jianning Li        Graz University of Technology and Medical University of
                                 Graz, Austria and University Hospital Essen, Germany

Jan Egger           Graz University of Technology and Medical University of
                                 Graz, Austria and University Hospital Essen, Germany

## Challenge Committee and Co-organizers

Michele R. Aizenberg     University of Nebraska Medical Center, USA
Victor Alves              University of Minho, Portugal
David G. Ellis            University of Nebraska Medical Center, USA
Oldřich Kodym          Brno University of Technology, Czech Republic
Karin Pistracher        Medical University of Graz, Austria
Michal Španěl          Brno University of Technology, Czech Republic
Gord von Campe       Medical University of Graz, Austria

## Sponsors

TESCAN 3DIM Joint Venture (https://www.tescan3dim.com/)

**CAMed**
Clinical additive manufacturing
for medical applications

CAMed: Clinical additive manufacturing for medical applications
(https://www.medunigraz.at/camed/)

## Acknowledgements

The challenge received the support of CAMed - Clinical additive manufacturing for medical applications (COMET K-Project 871132), which is funded by the Austrian Federal Ministry of Transport, Innovation and Technology (BMVIT), the Austrian Federal Ministry for Digital and Economic Affairs (BMDW), and the Styrian Business Promotion Agency (SFG). Furthermore, the challenge had the support of the Austrian Science Fund (FWF) KLI 678-B31: "enFaced: Virtual and Augmented Reality Training and Navigation Module for 3D-Printed Facial Defect Reconstructions". We also want to thank the Computer Algorithms for Medicine Laboratory (https://cafe-lab.org/) members and the paper reviewers. Finally, we thank Zhaodi Deng for the design of the original challenge logo.

# Contents

# Personalized Calvarial Reconstruction in Neurosurgery

Laurèl Rauschenbach[✉], Christoph Rieß, Ulrich Sure, and Karsten H. Wrede

Department of Neurosurgery and Spine Surgery, University Hospital Essen, Hufelandstrasse 55, 45147 Essen, Germany
laurel.rauschenbach@uk-essen.de

**Abstract.** Neurosurgical procedures often involve local skull bone removal to combat specific pathologies. Defect covering is mandatory in most cases and usually requires the application of bespoke and synthetically engineered implants. Since manufacturing management faces several barriers in the design, fabrication, and application process, there is an unmet need for improvement. In this article, the authors review the background of skull bone removal and calvarial reconstruction techniques, highlight the challenges on the horizon, and investigate future pathways.

**Keywords:** Craniectomy · Cranioplasty · Personalized medicine · Implant · Neurosurgery

## 1 Indications for Craniectomy

Craniectomy is the surgical removal of bone from the skull. In most cases, living with a cranial bone defect is temporary. In a follow-up surgery, the removed bone flap can either be reimplanted or the defect can be covered using synthetically manufactured implants [1, 2]. The reasons for craniectomy are manifold, involving numerous different pathologies.

Most commonly, craniectomy aims to decompress, relieving the mass effect of brain swelling and decreasing elevated intracranial pressure. Brain swelling constitutes a life-threatening emergency and is often the result of bleeding or edema deriving from infarction, traumatic brain injury, cerebral hypoxia, intracerebral hemorrhage, cerebral venous thrombosis, or encephalitis [3, 4]. Notably, the idea of decompressive craniectomy is not new. Centuries ago, Alexander Monro and George Kellie first described the relationship between intracranial content and intracranial pressure. After several revisions, this concept later became known as the Monro-Kellie doctrine [5]. This principle states that the sum of brain volume, intracranial cerebrospinal fluid, and intracranial blood must be constant to ensure an equilibrium of physiological intracranial pressure. An increase in one volume should cause a reciprocal decrease in the remaining components; Otherwise, the intracranial pressure will rise. Thus, brain swelling always displaces cerebrospinal fluid and blood out of the skull to create space. However, given the small volume of intracranial cerebrospinal fluid and blood, these compliance mechanisms are usually

© Springer Nature Switzerland AG 2021
J. Li and J. Egger (Eds.): AutoImplant 2021, LNCS 13123, pp. 1–7, 2021.
https://doi.org/10.1007/978-3-030-92652-6_1

exhausted quickly in the case of brain swelling and patients are regularly referred for neurosurgical treatment. Therapeutically, intracranial hypertension can only be released by draining cerebrospinal fluid, removing space occupying lesions, or removing bone from the skull to increase the available space.

Beside of decompression, there are other reasons for the removal of skull bone. Osteodestructive neoplastic lesions that arise within the bone or infiltrate bone structures require complete tumor resection to prevent recurrent tumor growth. Notably, bone tropism is a frequently occurring characteristic of numerous benign and malignant tumor entities, involving metastases, myeloma, meningioma, sarcoma, hemangioma, osteoma, Langerhans cell histiocytosis, or fibrous dysplasia [6]. Head injury with skull fractures also accounts for several skull bone defects. Particularly complex fractures sometimes require the removal of bone fragments, especially in the case of osseous contamination due to skin penetration.

Moreover, bone-associated infections usually demand craniectomy and permanent bone flap removal to eliminate the maintaining sources of inflammation. Lastly, patients with surgically reimplanted bone flaps can exhibit delayed and spontaneous bone resorption, usually resulting in painful skull deformation. In this case, the reimplanted flap must be removed, again resulting in a cranial defect.

## 2   Indications for Cranioplasty

Cranioplasty is the surgical repair of a bone defect following a previous craniectomy. Notably, skull bone reconstruction is not always mandatory, but most pathologies involve delayed covering of the defect. Different surgical techniques exist to restore the contour of the skull. On the one hand, the original bone can be reimplanted [1]. For this technique, the removed bone flap must be conserved directly after craniectomy, mainly using cryoconservation and less commonly by temporally implanting the skull flap into the anterior abdominal wall. On the other hand, the bone defect can be covered using custom contoured and alloplastic implants [2] (Fig. 1).

Cranioplasty might be performed for several reasons. The most apparent indication for covering a skull defect is protection. After craniectomy, the brain is covered by meninges, muscle, and scalp, but these layers only consist of soft tissues and do not adequately protect the brain from external forces. Moreover, most patients in good neurological condition demand restoration of the normal barriers protecting the intracranial structures for aesthetic reasons. After craniectomy, brain and soft tissue layers usually succumb to some sinking once the initial brain swelling has subsided, resulting in indentations and asymmetrical skull configuration (Fig. 2A). Given the prominent visibility of the head and the unique perception of the brain, many of the patients affected suffer from psychosocial disturbances and decreased quality of life. In this case, only cranioplasty can mitigate the individual's burden.

One of the major symptoms after cranioplasty and initial neurological recovery is headache located in the area of the removed bone flap [7]. Post-craniectomy headache is one of the most frequently reported adverse events, and depending on the severity of pain, these patients often require a combination of surgical calvarial reconstruction and analgesic drug treatment. The most urgent indication for cranioplasty is the sinking flap syndrome. Affected patients exhibit a severe concave, introflexed aspect of the craniectomy flap, and gradual neurological deterioration [8]. In this scenario, patients should be referred for surgery to restore the physiological anatomy and to allow neurological convalescence.

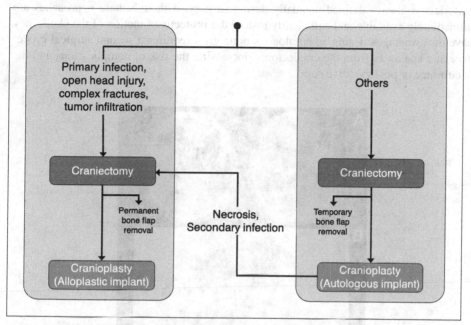

**Fig. 1.** Regular work flow for cranioplasty management using alloplastic implants (left) or autologous bone flaps (right). Infectious diseases, open head injuries with osseous contamination, complex fractures, intraosseous tumor growth or secondary bone flap necrosis inevitably require permanent bone flap removal and usage of alloplastic implants.

Defect covering is unnecessary in certain clinical scenarios. Firstly, minor defects do not necessarily require cranioplasty if the patient is satisfied and has no craniectomy-associated neurological deficit. Moreover, in patients with high risk of intraoperative or postoperative complications, such as in the case of severe comorbidities, anticoagulant medication, or history of delayed wound healing, decisions about cranioplasty must be taken carefully, and interests must be balanced with caution.

## 3  Personalized Calvarial Reconstruction

The physiological anatomy of the cranium can be reconstructed by autologous bone flap reimplantation (Fig. 2A) or insertion of a cranial implant that individually covers the bone defect (Fig. 2B, 2C). For the latter, several treatment approaches are available. These approaches can be classified according to the mode of production and the time of availability.

First, existing techniques allow immediate covering in the initial surgery, e.g., using autologous bone graft from the calvaria or iliac crest, bone cement, or titanium meshes. These reconstruction approaches are suitable for many patients unless the brain is swelling or the wound is infected (Fig. 3). However, reconstruction of skull defects with bone, cement, or titanium is technically challenging as the required shape of these materials is always defined manually during surgery. Although these approaches are immediately available and sufficiently restore the protective function of the skull, they have disadvantages. Using an autologous bone graft requires a second surgical procedure at a site away from the craniectomy, increasing the risk of complications and the occurrence of postoperative pain.

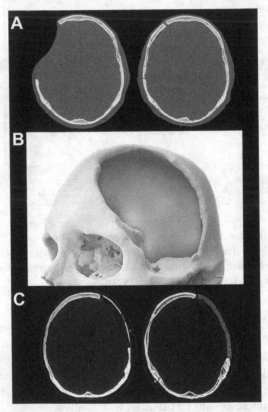

**Fig. 2.** Calvarial reconstruction techniques. (A) Computed tomography imaging with cranial bone defect following decompressive craniectomy (left) and after autologous bone flap reimplantation (right). (B) Printed three-dimensional model with cranial bone defect for custom-fit implant planning. (C) Postoperative computed tomography imaging after implantation of custom-fit implants.

Moreover, usage of autologous bone always carries the risk of spontaneous bone necrosis and, therefore, potential subsequent intervention. Finally, bone graft, cement, and titanium require intraoperative processing to ensure physiological alignment between cranium and implant. Since bone graft from the calvaria or iliac crest never represent skull anatomy appropriately, postoperative alterations in the shape of the calvarium are likely. Bone cement and titanium mesh are manually shaped by the surgeon and fixed to the skull bone. Here, the aesthetic outcome can vary from patient to patient and often remains unsatisfactory as it depends on the surgeon's experience and the extent of cranial bone defect.

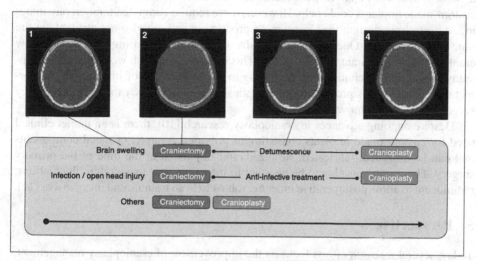

**Fig. 3.** Windows of opportunity for cranioplasty. Decompressive craniectomy for brain swelling and craniectomy for infection or osseous contamination due to skin penetration require time between craniectomy and cranioplasty. This is usually not the case for other diseases that require craniectomy. Here, defect covering might be performed in one surgery following skull bone removal. Note the computed tomography scans of one patient with increasing intracranial pressure (1), receiving decompressive craniectomy (2), revealing recovery of initial brain swelling (3) and finally admitted to cranioplasty (4).

On the other hand, there are existing custom-fit implants based on the patient's individual anatomy and rely on high resolution computed tomography scans made after craniectomy. Consequently, using these implants inevitably requires a second surgery, making this solution less attractive for patients with bone defects that could be covered immediately. Although these custom-made implants allow the perfect realization of personalized calvarial reconstruction and provide excellent alignment with the skull, this technique of cranioplasty is time-consuming and expensive. It has risks related to ionizing radiation due to the computed tomography scan. Today, several companies offer their service in producing patient-specific implants, fabricating them using milling or three-dimensional printing techniques. Available implants usually consist of hydroxyapatite, polyetheretherketone (PEEK), polymethylmethacrylate (PMMA), or titanium. Since the choice of material impacts biocompatibility, osteointegration, mechanical resistance, intraoperative workability, cosmetic outcome, radiolucency, infection rate, and cost, the use of each material widely varies depending on the clinical scenario and the neurosurgical department [2, 9].

## 4   Challenges and Requirements

Except for patients with brain swelling and infectious diseases, bone covering should be performed immediately after craniectomy to eliminate the need for subsequent surgery. In this scenario, only manually shaped implants can be used, involving bone graft, bone cement, or titanium meshes. These materials are cheap, often restore protection and to some extent skull anatomy, but often lack sufficient cosmetic repair. In this regard, custom-made implants could help. However, these require computed tomography imaging, out-of-clinic design, time-consuming production and are also not available at the time of first surgery. One might hypothesize that prefabricated implants could allow craniectomy concomitant to cranioplasty. This one-step approach would require preoperative definition of craniectomy according to the availability of implants of the correct size. Notably, this procedure is not applicable in most cases, especially emergency surgeries or tumor removal surgeries.

Despite ongoing advances in cranioplasty research [10], there is an unmet clinical need for custom-made implants consisting of polymer, ceramic, or metal components that can be designed, fabricated, sterilized, and implanted at the time of the primary surgery. These implants should be resistant to infections and temperature fluctuations, radiolucent to allow postoperative imaging, robust to head trauma, and inexpensive [11].

## 5   Perspective

Today, several research efforts focus on the improvement of cranioplasty management. The out-of-clinic approach currently applied is not suitable for patients who only require one surgery and consequently, there is a great need for onsite manufacturing facilities. One might hypothesize that the explanted bone flap could be used as a template for implant design, but this does not consider patients with non-physiological skull anatomy, e.g., patients with traumatic or neoplastic diseases. Moreover, mirroring the contralateral intact cranial site is often inadequate, as skull anatomy is not always symmetrical, and craniectomies can involve both sites. Alternative techniques are required that assess the extent of craniectomy, performing a three-dimensional analysis of the cranium. Here, intraoperative computed tomography imaging could help. Imaging could be done directly after craniectomy, allowing for intraoperative design, fabrication, and sterilization of an individual implant using mining or three-dimensional printing. However, intraoperative computed tomography imaging is rarely available, and the process of design, fabrication, and sterilization is time-consuming and currently takes several weeks. This process must be sped up to realize intraoperative implant applicability within several minutes. Here, artificial-intelligence-based computer-assisted design approaches and improved machine performance are inevitably needed. Moreover, development of new biomaterials for implant manufacturing is required, since certain aspects of fabrication must be sped up, for example, polymerization time. Moreover, competitive research attempts are currently investigating molecular strategies to induce osteogenesis and support bone healing. This might be interesting not only for autologous bone grafting techniques but also for next-generation, synthetically generated implants [2].

When it comes to craniectomy, these procedures are often followed by a second surgery that might be avoidable. Innovative solutions that allow personalized implant design within minutes are warranted. Considering the scope of challenges, this topic must be addressed interdisciplinarily with neurosurgeons, engineers, material scientists, biomedical scientists, and computer scientists [12].

# References

1. Sundseth, J., Sundseth, A., Berg-Johnsen, J., Sorteberg, W., Lindegaard, K.F.: Cranioplasty with autologous cryopreserved bone after decompressive craniectomy: complications and risk factors for developing surgical site infection. Acta neurochirurgica 156(4), 805–811 (2014). Discussion 11
2. Shah, A.M., Jung, H., Skirboll, S.: Materials used in cranioplasty: a history and analysis. Neurosurg. Focus 36(4), E19 (2014)
3. Changa, A.R., Czeisler, B.M., Lord, A.S.: Management of elevated intracranial pressure: a review. Current Neurol. Neurosci. Rep. 19(12), 1 (2019). https://doi.org/10.1007/s11910-019-1010-3
4. Jabbarli, R., et al.: Size does matter: the role of decompressive craniectomy extent for outcome after aneurysmal subarachnoid hemorrhage. Eur. J. Neurol. 28(7), 2200–2207 (2021)
5. Wilson, M.H.: Monro-Kellie 2.0: the dynamic vascular and venous pathophysiological components of intracranial pressure. J. Cereb. Blood Flow Metab. 36(8), 1338–1350 (2016). Official Journal of the International Society of Cerebral Blood Flow and Metabolism
6. Nakamura, H., Wang, H., Westesson, P.L., Hoshikawa, M., Takagi, M., Nakajima, Y.: Intraosseous tumors of the skull. Pic. Rev. Neuroradiol. J. 25(4), 461–468 (2012)
7. Haldar, R., Kaushal, A., Gupta, D., Srivastava, S., Singh, P.K.: Pain following craniotomy: reassessment of the available options. BioMed Res. Int. 2015, 509164 (2015)
8. Di Rienzo, A., et al.: Sinking flap syndrome revisited: the who, when and why. Neurosurg. Rev. 43(1), 323–335 (2019). https://doi.org/10.1007/s10143-019-01148-7
9. Piitulainen, J.M., Kauko, T., Aitasalo, K.M., Vuorinen, V., Vallittu, P.K., Posti, J.P.: Outcomes of cranioplasty with synthetic materials and autologous bone grafts. World Neurosurg. 83(5), 708–714 (2015)
10. Bonda, D.J., Manjila, S., Selman, W.R., Dean, D.: The recent revolution in the design and manufacture of cranial implants: modern advancements and future directions. Neurosurgery 77(5), 814–24 (2015). Discussion 24
11. Aydin, S., Kucukyuruk, B., Abuzayed, B., Aydin, S., Sanus, G.Z.: Cranioplasty: review of materials and techniques. J. Neurosci. Rural Pract. 2(2), 162–167 (2011)
12. von Campe, G., Pistracher, K.: Patient specific implants (PSI). In: Li, J., Egger, J. (eds.) AutoImplant 2020. LNCS, vol. 12439, pp. 1–9. Springer, Cham (2020). https://doi.org/10.1007/978-3-030-64327-0_1

# Qualitative Criteria for Feasible Cranial Implant Designs

David G. Ellis(✉) ⓘ, Carlos M. Alvarezⓘ, and Michele R. Aizenbergⓘ

Department of Neurosurgery, University of Nebraska Medical Center, Omaha, NE, USA
david.ellis@unmc.edu

**Abstract.** As part of the 2021 MICCAI AutoImplant Challenge, CT scans from 11 patients who had undergone cranioplasty using artificial implants were collected. Images of the reconstructed defective skulls before cranioplasty for these patients were shared with participating teams. Three teams submitted cranial implant designs. An experienced neurosurgeon evaluated the submissions to judge the feasibility of the implant designs for use in cranioplasty procedures. None of the submitted cranial implant designs were deemed feasible for use in cranioplasty procedures without modifications. While many implants adequately restored the skull shape by covering the defect area, most contained excess material outside of the defect, fit poorly within the defect and were too thick. Future research should move beyond solely restoring the skull shape and focus on designing implants that contain smooth transitions between skull and implant, cover the entire defect, contain no material outside of the defect, have minimal thickness, and are implantable.

**Keywords:** Cranial implant design · Cranioplasty · Dataset

## 1 Introduction

In 2020, the Medical Imaging Computing and Computer Assisted Intervention (MICCAI) Society hosted the AutoImplant Challenge to assess the best methods for automatically designing cranial implants [1]. The organizers designed the challenge around a dataset of skull images that contained artificial defects and corresponding implant images that filled in the artificial defects to restore the original unaltered skull. While the challenge resulted in numerous submitted solutions to automatically designing implants for artificial cases, the applicability of these methods to clinical cases remained unanswered.

For the 2021 AutoImplant Challenge, we sought to ascertain whether participating teams could design implants that neurosurgeons would deem feasible for use in cranioplasty procedures. To this end, the 2021 AutoImplant Challenge featured images of skulls with cranial defects from patients who underwent cranioplasty procedures at the University of Nebraska Medical Center. Challenge participants were invited to develop models based on the artificial datasets available in the challenge and then submit implant designs for each patient's defect. The implant designs were qualitatively evaluated by a neurosurgeon to determine if these implant designs could be used in a cranioplasty procedure.

J. Li and J. Egger (Eds.): AutoImplant 2021, LNCS 13123, pp. 8–18, 2021.
https://doi.org/10.1007/978-3-030-92652-6_2

In this article, we will outline the criteria we used to evaluate the designs of cranial implants and criteria that should be considered in the future. We will show exemplary cases where implant designs either fulfilled or failed to meet the qualitative standards for implant feasibility. We believe that the criteria outlined here can serve as a guide for future research looking to develop better automatic methods for producing feasible cranial implant designs.

## 2   Methods

### 2.1   Data

For the AutoImplant 2021 Challenge, we assembled scans from 11 patients who had undergone cranioplasty for acquired cranial defects. Each patient had a high-resolution CT scan of the skull before and after cranial reconstruction with an artificial implant. The post-cranioplasty CT scans were registered to the pre-implant scan using affine registrations [2]. Binary images of the skulls before cranioplasty were computed for each patient by applying a threshold of 150 Hounsfield Units to the image [3]. The post-cranioplasty scan was then used to guide the creation of a binary image of the cranial implant design. This process included selectively thresholding the defect area above 100 Hounsfield units and removing any voxels resulting from noise from imaging and interpolation artifacts.

### 2.2   Evaluation

For Task 2 of the AutoImplant 2021 Challenge, participants were given the binary images of the skulls and asked to submit binary images of implant designs based upon their automatic implant design methods. The submitted implant images were qualitatively evaluated by an experienced neurosurgeon (MRA). In order to perform the evaluations, the skull images and the predicted implant images from the submissions were converted to surface models in 3D Slicer (www.slicer.org) [4]. The implant predictions were judged based on false positive area, completeness, fit, and overall implant feasibility (Table 1). Completeness was defined as the amount of the defect area covered by the implant. False positive area was defined as the amount of implant outside of the defect area. Fit was defined as whether or not the shape and profile of the implant design matched the defect. Finally, the overall implant feasibility judged whether or not the implant design could be used in a cranioplasty procedure.

The submitted implant images were also quantitatively evaluated against the implant images derived from the post-cranioplasty CT scans. The metrics used for the quantitative evaluation were dice similarity coefficient (DSC), boundary DSC (bDSC), and 95% Hausdorff distance (HD95).

### 2.3   3D Printing

For an exemplary subject, a submitted implant design from each team was converted from their native file format to STL. The submission STL files were then sliced using

**Table 1.** Evaluation criteria used to judge the submitted implant designs.

| Completeness | False positive area | Fit | Overall implant feasibility |
|---|---|---|---|
| 100% | None | Yes | Feasible with no flaws |
| >75% | Minimal | No | Feasible with some minor flaws |
| >50% | Moderate | | Feasible with minimal modifications |
| >25% | Gross | | Feasible with significant modifications |
| <25% | | | Not feasible |

Makerbot Print (New York, NY) software with a layer thickness of 0.1 mm. Finally, the submissions were printed using polylactic acid (PLA) filament and a Polyvinyl Alcohol (PVA) dissolvable support material on a Makerbot Method (Makerbot New York, NY) printer. The support material was then dissolved using water over 24 h, yielding the final product.

## 3  Results

### 3.1  Qualitative Analysis

We received five submissions for our task (Task 2) in the AutoImplant 2021 Challenge. One of the submissions could not be evaluated because the origin was incorrectly set in the image header. qualitative evaluation was performed on the remaining four submissions.

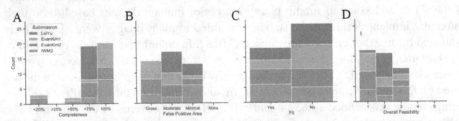

**Fig. 1.** Distribution of qualitative evaluation scores for the 4 reviewed submissions. Distributions are shown for Completeness (A), False Positive Area (B), Fit (C), and Overall Feasibility (D). Most of the submissions were deemed to be either complete or nearly complete. All submissions were deemed to have some amount of false positive area. The majority of the submissions did not fit the defect area. Overall, none of the submissions were deemed to be feasible for im-plantation without needing prior modifications.

### Completeness

We defined completeness as the amount of the defect area covered by the implant. Thus, completeness is related to the sensitivity of the submissions to design an implant to cover the entire defect area accurately. Encouragingly, most of the implants were greater than 75% complete, as shown in Fig. 1A. However, all implant submissions did not accurately cover the defect area for a patient with a very large defect (Fig. 2, left). Additionally, some implant designs had small sections missing around the edge of the defect area (Fig. 2, right). While these sections should be included in the implant design, small sections such as the one shown are unlikely to drastically affect the implant design's usability.

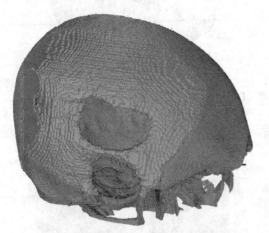 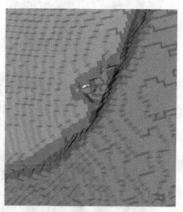

**Fig. 2.** Examples of incomplete implant designs. All of the submissions had difficulty designing implants for large defects (left). There were also some cases where the implant designs were missing small areas on the border of the defect (right).

### False Positive Area

We defined false positive area as the amount of implant outside of the defect area. Thus, false positive area is related to the specificity of the implant design to include only locations within the defect area. All of the implant design submissions had some amount of false positive area (Fig. 1B). Figure 3 shows examples of false positive areas from submitted implant designs. We noticed that in some cases, implant designs focused on the incorrect defect area, such as the removed facial bones or more minor defects from previous surgeries. Examples such as shown in Fig. 3A were partially due to participants' models targeting the facial bones removed for anonymization purposes. Examples such as shown in Fig. 3B were the result of predicting both the correct defect area as well as additional defect areas. Figure 3C shows an implant design with a profile that does not match the desired shape for an implant. The false positive area, in this case, extends out beyond the defect area. Figure 3D shows a small area included in an implant design underneath the skull and outside of the defect area.

### Fit

We defined the implant designs' fit as whether the implant design's shape and profile matched the defect and skull. As shown in Fig. 1C, the majority of the implant designs did not have the correct profile and shape. However, this is likely due to the overlap of the fit category with the false positive area and completeness categories. Intuitively, implant designs that are incomplete or contain areas outside of the defect area are unlikely to match the shape and profile of the defect area. Figure 4 gives an example of a submitted implant design with poor fit to the defect area.

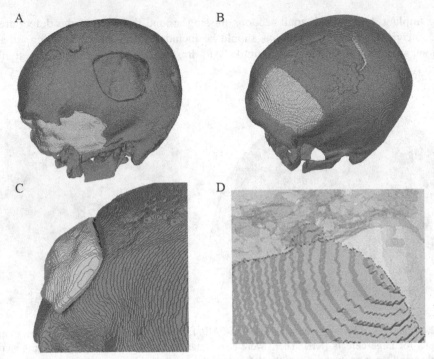

**Fig. 3.** Examples of different types of false positive area included in submitted designs. Some implant designs focused on the incorrect area. (A) shows an implant design that attempts to restore part of the facial bones that were removed for anonymization purposes. (B) shows an implant design that includes defect area from a previous surgery. (C) shows an implant design with false positive area that extends out from the defect area. (D) shows a small area that was included in the implant design underneath the skull and outside of the defect area.

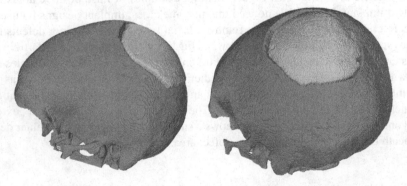

**Fig. 4.** Example of an implant design with poor fit to the defect area.

**Overall Implant Feasibility**

We used the overall implant feasibility score to judge whether the implant design could be used in a cranioplasty procedure. Unfortunately, none of the submitted implant designs were deemed feasible without modifications. The main issues affecting implant feasibility were due to poor compliance with the outlined criteria above (completeness, false positive area, and fit). Additionally, it was noted that the majority submitted implant designs matched the thickness of the skull, which made them too thick to be used in a cranioplasty procedure. Thick implants make implantation difficult and may overly compress brain and scar tissue. Feasible cranial implants maintain tensile strength equal to or exceeding that of the skull while being thin enough to implant safely. In many cases, the ideal thickness for implants may be less than 50% of the skull thickness.

## 3.2  Quantitative Analysis

The submitted implant designs were also evaluated against the binary implant images from the post-cranioplasty CT scans for HD95, DSC, and bDSC. Figure 5 shows the distribution of the quantitative scores for the submitted methods. compared to quantitative scores from the AutoImplant 2020 Challenge evaluated using artificial defects and implants, the quantitative scores are poor [5, 6]. We can identify three reasons why the scores might be worse compared to the scores evaluated against the artificial implant designs. First, as detailed in the qualitative analysis results section, there are many problems with the implant design submissions, such as false positive areas and incomplete implant designs. Looking at Fig. 6, we can see that the quantitative metrics are moderately correlated [7] to most of the qualitative evaluation metrics. Therefore, we expect that the issues outlined in the qualitative evaluations account for a significant portion, but probably not all of the deviation from the high scores that we have seen on other datasets. Second, the implants used in the patient cranioplasty cases are much thinner than the skull making the match between the submitted implant designs and the actual designs poor. Lastly, metal (titanium cranial fixation plates and screws) used in the cranioplasty procedure produced CT imaging artifacts may have distorted the true shape of the implant. We believe that all three of these problems are contributing to the relatively poor quantitative metrics.

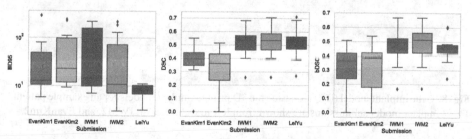

**Fig. 5.** Quantitative evaluation scores of the submitted implant designs compared to the implanted designs reconstructed from the post-cranioplasty CT scans.

## 3.3  Evaluation of 3D Printed Implant Designs

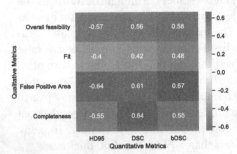

**Fig. 6.** Pearson correlations between the quantitative and qualitative evaluation metrics. Overall, the quantitative metrics are moderately correlated to the qualitative metrics. This indicates that there is some variance in the quantitative metrics that is not captured by the qualitative evaluations.

We selected an implant design from each team for a defective skull from one of the patients for whom we had a model of the defective skull (Fig. 7) and the implant used in the cranioplasty procedure (Fig. 8). We then compared the shape, thickness, and profile of the submitted implant models to that of the model for the actual implant. In Fig. 8, we can see that the thickness of the actual implant model is much thinner than that of any of the submitted implant models. Furthermore, we can see that the IWM2 model has a concave shape with some material that may overlap both underneath and overtop the skull.

In Fig. 9, the fit and profile of the implant models when placed onto the skull model are visualized. The model of the actual implant fits well in the defect area and has a smooth profile that transitions well from the skull to the implant. By comparison, the LeiYu model fits well and does not extend beyond the defect, but it does not have as smooth of a transition. The IWM2 model was unable to be implanted into the skull model due to its concave edges. Finally, the EvanKim2 model was able to be implanted but extended well beyond the desirable skull shape.

**Fig. 7.** Model of the defective skull for an example patient. The implant design submissions were 3D printed for this patient and evaluated using this skull model.

**Fig. 8.** True implant model (left) alongside the 3D printed implant models for an example patient. The 3 implant model submissions are shown from left to right: LeiYu, IWM2, and EvanKim2.

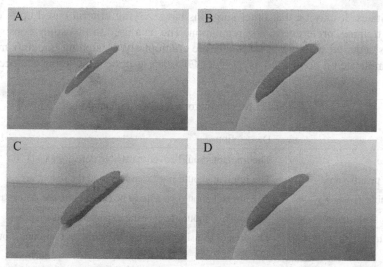

**Fig. 9.** Implant models placed onto the model of the defective skull to evaluate implantability and profile. (A) shows the model for the implant that was professionally designed and used in the cranioplasty procedure. We can see that the implant model does not extend beyond the skull and has smooth transitions from the skull to the implant. (B) shows the LeiYu implant model. Similar to A, the LeiYu model does not extend beyond the skull, but the transitions from the skull to the implant are not as smooth. (C) shows the IWM2 implant model. This implant model was not able to be implanted into the skull model due to the shape of its edges. (D) shows the implant model for EvanKim2. This implant model extends out from the defect area beyond the normal skull shape.

## 4 Discussion

Our analysis of the implant designs submitted as part of the AutoImplant 2021 Challenge shows that more progress needs to be made to achieve automatic implant designs that are feasible for use in cranioplasty cases. We found that while the submitted methods had reasonable sensitivity to the defect area, they often lacked the required specificity, thickness, shape, and smoothness.

Following these observations, in Table 2, we compiled a more extensive list of criteria that we believe constitute an ideal implant design. According to our criteria, the ideal implant will cover the entire defect area while not extending beyond it. An obvious but perhaps overlooked criterion is that the implant should be shaped to allow insertion into the defect area. Further, the implant should restore the expected skull shape and maintain smooth transitions between the skull and the implant. An implant that extrudes beyond the defect area may put unwanted pressure on the scalp resulting in tissue breakdown. Finally, the implant should be thin enough to facilitate placement without the surgeon needing to dissect extensively to avoid placing too much pressure on the underlying tissue (epidural scar and brain) but thick enough to provide appropriate tensile strength similar to or in excess of native bone. Thus, the ideal thickness depends on the size of the defect area and the material being used to manufacture the implant.

It should be noted that these criteria are based upon the clinical standards and practices of MRA and colleagues at the University of Nebraska Medical Center in the

United States. It may be that other surgeons have varying criteria based upon differences in training, preferences, and regulation. The data used in this study consisted of CT scans acquired within 1–3 weeks before cranioplasty. Designing implants may be more complicated if conducted using older CT scans as bone remodeling can occur.

**Table 2.** Qualitative criteria for a feasible implant design.

| Criteria | Description |
| --- | --- |
| Complete | The implant should cover the whole defect area |
| No false positive area | The implant should not extend beyond the defect area |
| Implantable | The implant should be able to be placed into the defect area |
| Restores skull shape | The implant should restore the expected skull shape |
| Smooth transition with skull | The area of transition between the skull and implant should be smooth |
| Minimal thickness | The implant must be thin enough as not to overly compress underlying tissue. Ideally, the implant should be at least 50% thinner than the skull |

[a]In cases of relatively thin skull thickness the implant may need to be close to the same thickness of the skull to maintain the necessary implant strength.

The primary reason that the implant design submissions were not feasible for real cranioplasty cases is due to the applicability of the available training sets. All participating teams used deep learning models to predict the desired implant shape. The data used to train the deep learning models consisted of artificial implants and defects derived from non-defective skulls. The artificial implants were simply sections of the skull that had been digitally removed from the skull image. Thus, the models were trained to predict implants as thick as the skull. As mentioned previously, we do not believe that implants with the same thickness as the skull are feasible for cranioplasty procedures. Therefore, we believe that the data openly available for this task does not fully suit the needs for automatic cranial implant design.

Additional research is needed to move from a simple skull completion objective to a more intricate implant design objective. It might be beneficial to define the implant design as a two-step process. The first step is to complete the skull and restore its original shape. This step is the focus of the available public datasets. The second step is to use the completed skull combined with the defective skull to determine the ideal implant shape. As previous work has shown, deep learning models are highly effective at performing the skull completion step [1, 5, 6, 8, 9]. Performing this step alone may save a significant amount of time in the implant design process. Moving from the first step to the second step by designing the ideal implant based on the completed skull may require image or morphological processing and analysis techniques as ground truth data for this task is not yet available. These more traditional methods may be advantageous for this task as they could allow the implant design to be easily modified to meet varying thickness requirements based on the type of implant material being used and the size of the defect.

Alternatively, manually annotated datasets could be produced to allow models to be trained to mimic expert implant designs.

We would like to mention that our results are not representative of the entire field of automatic implant design but only of the submissions to our task in the AutoImplant 2021 Challenge. Other researchers, including some of the challenge organizers, have done extensive previous work [8, 9] but did not submit their models for evaluation. Their trained models may prove to produce closer to feasible implant designs than those evaluated in this study.

We would also like to acknowledge that the submitted methods may perform better on clinical datasets that do not have their facial bones removed. We removed the facial bones out of an abundance of caution to maintain our patients' privacy. However, methods implemented in a clinical setting would not have to account for the removal of facial bones. Future work could be done to anonymize the facial bone features without removing them entirely.

## 5  Conclusion

When evaluated by an experienced neurosurgeon, none of the submitted cranial implant designs were deemed feasible for use in cranioplasty procedures without modifications. While many of the implants adequately restored the skull shape by covering the defect area, most contained excess material outside of the defect, had poor fit with the defect, and were too thick. Future research should move beyond solely restoring the skull shape and additionally focus on designing implants that contain smooth transitions between skull and implant, cover the entire defect, contain no material outside of the defect, have minimal thickness, and are implantable.

## References

1. Li, J., Egger, J.: Towards the Automatization of Cranial Implant Design in Cranioplasty. Springer, Cham (2020). https://doi.org/10.1007/978-3-030-64327-0
2. Avants, B.B., Tustison, N., Song, G.: Advanced normalization tools (ANTS). Insight J 2(365), 1–35 (2009)
3. Kodym, O., et al.: SkullBreak/SkullFix–Dataset for automatic cranial implant design and a benchmark for volumetric shape learning tasks. Data Brief 35, 106902 (2021)
4. Kikinis, R., Pieper, S., Vosburgh, K.: 3D slicer: a platform for subject-specific image analysis, visualization, and clinical support. In: Jolesz, F.A. (ed.) Intraoperative Imaging and Image-Guided Therapy, pp. 277–289. Springer, New York (2014). https://doi.org/10.1007/978-1-4614-7657-3_19
5. Li, J., et al.: AutoImplant 2020-first MICCAI challenge on automatic cranial implant design. IEEE Trans. Med. Imaging 40(9), 2329–2342 (2021)
6. Ellis, D., Aizenberg, M.: Deep learning using augmentation via registration: 1st place solution to the autoimplant 2020 challenge. In: Li, J., Egger, J. (eds.) AutoImplant. LNCS, vol. 12439, pp. 47–55. Springer, Cham (2020). https://doi.org/10.1007/978-3-030-64327-0_6
7. Mukaka, M.M.: Statistics corner: a guide to appropriate use of correlation coefficient in medical research. Malawi Med. J. J. Med. Assoc. Malawi 24(3), 69–71 (2012)

18      D. G. Ellis et al.

8. Kodym, O., Španěl, M., Herout, A.: Deep learning for cranioplasty in clinical practice: going from synthetic to real patient data. Comput. Biol. Med. **137**, 104766 (2021)
9. Li, J., et al.: Automatic skull defect restoration and cranial implant generation for cranioplasty. Med. Image Anal. **73**, 102171 (2021)

# Segmentation of Defective Skulls from CT Data for Tissue Modelling

Oldřich Kodym[1]([✉]), Michal Španěl[1,2], and Adam Herout[1]

[1] Graph@FIT, Brno University of Technology, Brno, Czech Republic
ikodym@fit.vutbr.cz, spanel@t3d.team
[2] TESCAN 3DIM, Brno, Czech Republic

**Abstract.** In this work we present a method of automatic segmentation of defective skulls for custom cranial implant design and 3D printing purposes. Since such tissue models are usually required in patient cases with complex anatomical defects and variety of external objects present in the acquired data, most deep learning-based approaches fall short because it is not possible to create a sufficient training dataset that would encompass the spectrum of all possible structures. Because CNN segmentation experiments in this application domain have been so far limited to simple patch-based CNN architectures, we first show how the usage of the encoder-decoder architecture can substantially improve the segmentation accuracy. Then, we show how the number of segmentation artifacts, which usually require manual corrections, can be further reduced by adding a boundary term to CNN training and by globally optimizing the segmentation with graph-cut. Finally, we show that using the proposed method, 3D segmentation accurate enough for clinical application can be achieved with 2D CNN architectures as well as their 3D counterparts.

**Keywords:** Computed tomography · Pre-surgical planning · Segmentation · Convolutional neural networks · Graph-cut

## 1 Introduction

Computer-assisted pre-surgical planning using generated 3D tissue models is seeing increasing use in personalized medicine [14]. In the context of craniofacial surgery, the applications range from patient education, diagnosis and operative planning [1] to patient-specific implant design [3], mostly in the cranial area. The latter had been accelerated by the advent of additive manufacturing (AM), also known as 3D printing in recent years [2]. A typical workflow of producing a pre-surgical 3D tissue model consists of data acquisition, converting the data into patient model and optionally printing the model. Computed tomography (CT) is usually the modality of choice because of its unparalleled hard tissue contrast required for precise model shape extraction. As the manufacturing process is usually able to produce the model with a satisfactory precision, converting the raw CT data into an accurate patient model remains the most crucial step [4].

© Springer Nature Switzerland AG 2021
J. Li and J. Egger (Eds.): AutoImplant 2021, LNCS 13123, pp. 19–28, 2021.
https://doi.org/10.1007/978-3-030-92652-6_3

Precise segmentation of the patient skull is therefore critical. Although simple global thresholding followed by laborious post-processing and cleaning remains the most commonly used method in medical AM [5], numerous semi- or fully automatic methods have been proposed for skull segmentation. Cuadros et al. [12] used super-voxels followed by clustering and the level-set method has been applied to new-born skull segmentation in CT by Ghadimi et al. [13]. Following the success of the convolutional neural networks (CNN) in biomedical segmentation for both 2D [7] and 3D [8,9] settings, Minnema et al. used a simple patch-wise CNN for segmentation of skulls with defects for AM [11]. However, so far none of these methods have been able to show evidence that they are robust enough to be implemented into medical practice.

In this work, we propose an improved segmentation method that extracts region and boundary potentials using CNN and then uses graph-cut for globally optimal segmentation. The method outperforms methods based on conventional deep learning and other state-of-the-art methods of skull segmentation, and it produces results acceptable for the targeted use of 3D tissue modelling in the clinical practice. Furthermore, we directly compare 2D and 3D CNNs for segmentation and demonstrate that the benefit of using the 3D approach is not unequivocal.

## 2   Proposed Method

We use the well known U-net model [7] as a baseline method for our segmentation experiments. We experimented with both multi-view (MV) ensemble of 3 orthogonal 2D U-nets as used in [10] and fully 3D U-net [8] since to authors' best knowledge, the current literature lacks direct comparison between the two approaches. The applied U-net slightly differs from the original architecture by using batch normalization and padding during convolutions, replacing the up-conv layers with bilinear up-sampling and reducing the initial number of convolutions to 16. The architecture of the 3D model is identical except that each convolution, max-pooling, and up-sampling operation is replaced by its 3D equivalent. The networks are trained until convergence using mini batches of shape $24 \times 128 \times 128$ in case of 2D and $4 \times 128 \times 128 \times 64$ in case of 3D model using the Dice loss function [9].

To improve segmentation performance on slightly out-of-distribution data (such as previously unseen medical material or defect shapes), we opted to apply 3D graph-cut segmentation on the CNN output. While this approach has been taken by other authors before [16], we also modify our CNN model to output an edge probability for each voxel in addition to the object probability. Thus, the final layer of the CNN has 3 channels instead of the standard 2. Figure 2 illustrates how this step can provide additional boundary information to the graph-cut in comparison to simply using the conventional intensity or probability gradient. Another advantage of this approach is that since both region and boundary terms have similar dynamic range, finding optimal $\lambda$ parameter of the graph-cut algorithm is simplified. We leave $\lambda = 1$ throughout our experiments.

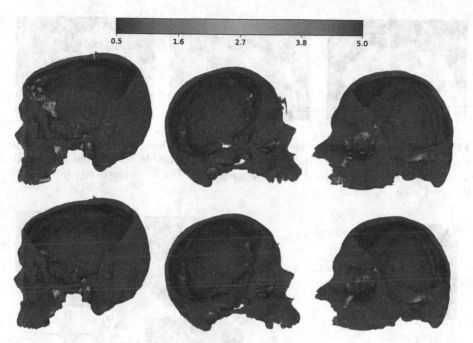

**Fig. 1.** Example renders of segmented skulls with the distance to the ground-truth surface in mm coded in color. Multi-view CNN segmentation outputs (top) and multi-view CutCNN segmentation outputs (bottom) are shown. To better display the differences, voxels with surface error of less than 0.5 mm are left dark blue.

We train the network using the following form of the Dice loss function:

$$\mathcal{L} = 1 - 2 \cdot \frac{\sum_{m=1}^{M} \left( p_0^m g_0^m + p_1^m g_1^m + p_e^m g_e^m \right)}{\sum_{m=1}^{M} \left( p_0^m + g_0^m + p_1^m + g_1^m + p_e^m + g_e^m \right)}, \tag{1}$$

where $p_0^m$ and $p_1^m$ are the probabilities of voxel $m$ belonging to class background and object respectively, and $g_0^m$ and $g_1^m$ are the corresponding ground-truth labels. Analogously, $p_e^m$ and $g_e^m$ are the probability and the ground-truth label of voxel belonging to the object edge. Edge map ground truth is obtained by subtracting the binary object from its morphologically dilated version, leaving a surface with single voxel thickness. Note that edge voxels overlap with the background voxels and the edge probability channel is therefore not included in the final softmax activation layer of the CNN.

Next, the output maps are converted into a 6-connected graph structure with the region terms $R\left(a\right)$ for voxel $a$ given by

$$R^{obj}(a) = -ln(p_1^a), \quad R^{bkg}(a) = -ln(p_0^a) \tag{2}$$

and the boundary term $B\left(a,b\right)$ between neighbouring voxels $a$ and $b$ given by

$$B(a,b) = -ln[max(p_e^a, p_e^b)]. \tag{3}$$

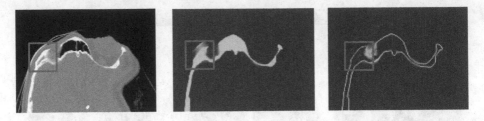

**Fig. 2.** Example CNN output slice, from left to right: Data, object probability map, edge probability map. Notice the segmentation error caused by an external object with density similar to that of the skull in upper left. The error is correctly separated by its detected edge.

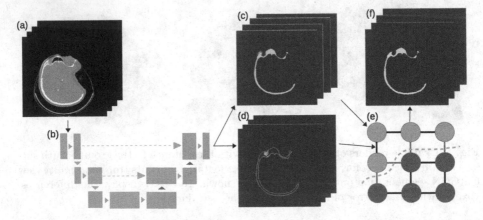

**Fig. 3.** Scheme of the proposed segmentation framework. Input data (a) are processed by a CNN model (b) to produce a probability map (c) and an edge strength map (d). These provide the boundary and region term for the graph-cut optimization step (e) which produces the binary output segmentation (f).

Finally, globally optimal 3D segmentation can be obtained by finding minimum cut through this graph [6]. This method will be referred to as CutCNN in the remaining parts of the paper. Note that while the CNN can be either MV (multi-view) or 3D, the graph-cut segmentation is always 3D. The method is summarized in Fig. 3.

## 3   Experiments

In this section, we present the skull tissue dataset on which the segmentation methods were evaluated. Then, we present the results of different segmentation methods on the dataset.

## 3.1   Dataset

Head CT scans of 199 different patients were available for this study. The scans were acquired for the purpose of patient skull modelling and its additive manufacturing or further patient-specific implant design. Therefore, pixel-wise ground-truth segmentation done by an experienced radiologist were also available for model training. The scans were acquired on multiple CT scanners using a variety of different acquisition protocols. The voxel size varied from $0.38 \times 0.38 \times 0.38$ mm to $0.5 \times 0.5 \times 1.5$ mm. All volumes were re-sampled to isometric resolution of 1 mm per voxel for the ablation experiments.

As the majority of these scans were acquired prior to a surgery, the skulls often contained various defects, fixation materials and other external objects. This makes fully automatic segmentation of these scans a challenging task, because many of these structures were only present in a single patient scan, making generalization difficult.

## 3.2   Metrics

Multiple metrics were used to quantitatively compare outputs of different segmentation methods used in the study. Inspired by the MICCAI 2018 Medical Segmentation Decathlon challenge [17], volumetric Dice coefficient and surface Dice coefficient were chosen. Furthermore, mean surface distance has been also included in the metrics as this is the recommended measure in area of medical tissue model preparation [5]. Implementations of the metrics used in this work are publicly available[1].

Dice coefficient (DC) is a well-known metric in medical segmentation domain. Given a number of true positive (TP) samples, false positive (FP) samples and false negative (FN) samples, the coefficient is given by

$$DC = \frac{2 \cdot TP}{2 \cdot TP + FP + FN}. \tag{4}$$

In case of volumetric Dice coefficient, number of voxels assigned an object label in output segmentation as well as in the ground-truth segmentation is used to compute TP while FP + FN correspond to the number of voxels assigned a different label.

To compute a surface Dice coefficient, the output and the ground-truth binary segmentation volumes are converted to polygon meshes. Each surface element in the output segmentation mesh is then considered a TP sample if the distance to the closest point on ground-truth surface is lower than threshold $t$ and vice-versa. The surface elements in output and ground-truth meshes that do not fall under this threshold are counted as FN and FP, respectively. We chose the threshold to correspond to the voxel size in our experiment.

---

[1] https://github.com/deepmind/surface-distance.

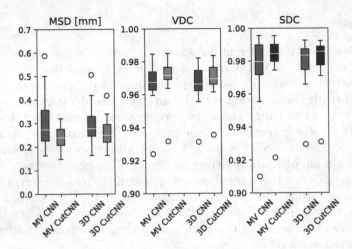

**Fig. 4.** Accuracy of standard multi-view (MV) and 3D CNN and their CutCNN counterparts. Results shown in terms of mean surface distance (MSD), volumetric Dice coefficient (VDC) and surface Dice coefficient (SDC).

### 3.3 Experimental Design and Results

Performance of four different models has been evaluated in this study. Both 3D and MV CNN models and their CutCNN counterparts have been implemented in the TensorFlow framework. PyMaxflow library has been used for implementation of the graph-cut optimization. All experiments were run on a desktop system equipped with Nvidia Titan Xp GPU, an i5 intel core processor and 16 GB RAM.

22 scans were randomly selected as test subjects for the experiment, leaving 177 skulls for model training. Using convolutional kernels of size 3 in all the CNN models results in the 3D model having the same number of trainable parameters as the sum of the three orthogonal 2D models. The comparison between the MV ensemble and the 3D approach can therefore be considered an ablation study to an extent. CutCNN models also have a similar number of parameters, the only

**Table 1.** Comparison of segmentation methods using mean surface distance (MSD) [mm], volumetric Dice coefficient (VDC) and surface Dice coefficient (SDC).

| Method | MSD | VDC | SDC |
|---|---|---|---|
| MV CNN | 0.37 | 96.7 | 97.1 |
| 3D CNN | 0.35 | 96.7 | 97.0 |
| MV CutCNN | **0.31** | 97.7 | **98.3** |
| 3D CutCNN | 0.32 | **98.0** | 98.1 |
| * Minnema et al. [11] | 0.44 | 92.0 | - |
| * Linares et al. [12] | - | 91.5 | - |

\* Results obtained on different datasets

difference being the final edge probability output layer. Quantitative comparison of results of each method are presented in Fig. 4 and Table 1. Further qualitative results are shown in Fig. 5 and 1.

# 4 Discussion

CutCNN segmentation framework resulted in a performance gain in all cases in terms of every metric used in the experiment over standard CNN approaches. The output of CNN object probability map often contains errors near external objects or smaller tissue defects as these are scarce in the training data distribution. However, the graph-cut optimization guides the resulting binary segmentation towards a spatially consistent and compact shape, often eliminating these artifacts if a detected edge corresponds mostly to the correct object boundary. This effect is further illustrated in Fig. 1.

Our second observation is that using 3D convolutional kernels has a rather small effect on the final segmentation precision quantitatively compared to the MV approach. However, although the quantitative difference is small, for applications in medical additive manufacturing, it is important to avoid ragged segmentation output which may result from MV CNN in areas of lower model certainty. These include for example teeth, which are challenging to detect, especially when the lower and upper teeth are in contact (see Fig. 5 a), or maxillary sinus, which is often enclosed in order to improve mechanical stability of the manufactured model (see Fig. 5 b). Therefore, 3D U-nets are often considered necessary to avoid these discontinuities caused by slice-by-slice processing.

However, this artifact can also be addressed by employing the CutCNN framework since ragged segmentation boundary introduces a high boundary-term penalization during optimization and it is therefore avoided in the final binary segmentation. Thus, employing CutCNN allows the decision between 3D or multi-view approach to be merely a technical choice. Using 2D models can offer some advantages, such as faster training of deeper models with less overfitting [10].

We also evaluate the performance of the proposed method in the context of existing related work in skull segmentation. In terms of volumetric Dice coefficient, the proposed method achieved performance of $0.977 \pm 0.019$ in the multi-view scenario and $0.980 \pm 0.013$ in the 3D scenario. This result is considerably higher than that of $0.92 \pm 0.04$ reported by Minnema et al. [11]. This is probably caused by the lower resolution in our experiments and by several limiting factors in the other works, including the small training set that only allowed for a smaller CNN architecture and employing a patch-based approach. To our best knowledge, the presented work is the first to apply a fully automatic segmentation approach to a pathological skull dataset of this size. Furthermore, we also achieve a low mean surface distance with the proposed method, namely $0.31 \pm 0.33$ mm.

We also trained the multi-view CutCNN model with isometric resolution of 0.5 mm per voxel to facilitate enough precision for clinical practice with almost

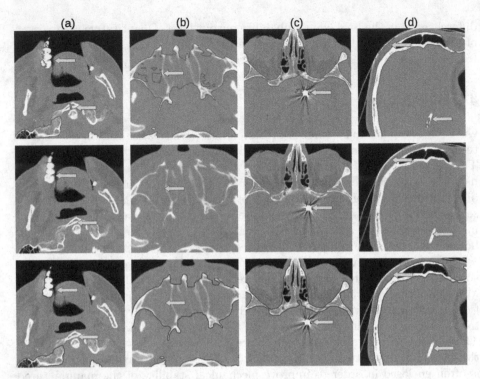

**Fig. 5.** Qualitative results shown for several chosen axial slices. From top to bottom: Multi-view CNN output (red), ground-truth (magenta), multi-view CutCNN output (blue). (Color figure online)

no loss in accuracy. Preliminary testing of the proposed method by experts in medical tissue modelling practice showed that the results of this model are accurate enough to substantially reduce the amount of time spent by creating the model in practice when compared to currently used semi-automatic segmentation methods.

## 5    Conclusions

In this work, we presented CutCNN, an improved hard tissue segmentation method which integrates the CNN output with graph-cut segmentation. The results of such a method surpassed the commonly used CNN architectures such as 3D and multi-view U-nets as well as other competitive methods in the skull segmentation domain. The object and edge probability maps in combination with graph cut provide a compact and smooth final tissue segmentation while adding very little computational cost. This method could therefore be used to improve the performance of any semantic segmentation task given that the edges are well defined in the data. In the future, to deal with any remaining segmentation errors, user interaction can be introduced to the method on both CNN and graph-cut level as the output of both steps can be improved through user scribbles in an iterative fashion. This will further reduce the time spent producing accurate tissue model.

**Acknowledgements.** This work was supported in part by the company TESCAN 3DIM. We also gratefully acknowledge the support of the NVIDIA Corporation with the donation of one NVIDIA TITAN Xp GPU for this research.

# References

1. D'Urso, P., et al.: Stereolithographic biomodelling in cranio-maxillofacial surgery: a prospective trial. J. Cranio-Maxillof. Surg. **27**(1), 30–37 (1999)
2. Mitsouras, D., et al.: Medical 3D printing for the radiologist. RadioGraphics. **35**(7), 1965–1988 (2015)
3. Jardini, A., et al.: Cranial reconstruction: 3D biomodel and custom-built implant created using additive manufacturing. J. Cranio-Maxillof. Surg. **42**(8), 1877–1884 (2014)
4. Martelli, N., et al.: Advantages and disadvantages of 3-dimensional printing in surgery: a systematic review. Surgery **159**(6), 1485–1500 (2016)
5. van Eijnatten, M., et al.: CT image segmentation methods for bone used in medical additive manufacturing. Med. Eng. Phys. **51**, 6–16 (2018)
6. Boykov, Y., Jolly, M.: Interactive graph cuts for optimal boundary & region segmentation of objects in N-D images. In: Proceedings of Eighth IEEE International Conference on Computer Vision (ICCV) (2001)
7. Ronneberger, O., Fischer, P., Brox, T.: U-Net: convolutional networks for biomedical image segmentation. In: Navab, N., Hornegger, J., Wells, W.M., Frangi, A.F. (eds.) MICCAI 2015. LNCS, vol. 9351, pp. 234–241. Springer, Cham (2015). https://doi.org/10.1007/978-3-319-24574-4_28
8. Çiçek, Ö., Abdulkadir, A., Lienkamp, S.S., Brox, T., Ronneberger, O.: 3D U-Net: learning dense volumetric segmentation from sparse annotation. In: Ourselin, S., Joskowicz, L., Sabuncu, M.R., Unal, G., Wells, W. (eds.) MICCAI 2016. LNCS, vol. 9901, pp. 424–432. Springer, Cham (2016). https://doi.org/10.1007/978-3-319-46723-8_49
9. Milletari, F., et al.: V-Net: fully convolutional neural networks for volumetric medical image segmentation. In: 2016 Fourth International Conference on 3D Vision (3DV) (2016)
10. Chen, Y., et al.: Hippocampus segmentation through multi-view ensemble ConvNets. In: Proceedings of IEEE 14th International Symposium on Biomedical Imaging (ISBI) (2017)
11. Minnema, J., et al.: CT image segmentation of bone for medical additive manufacturing using a convolutional neural network. Comput. Biol. Med. **103**, 130–139 (2018)
12. Cuadros Linares, O., Bianchi, J., Raveli, D., Batista Neto, J., Hamann, B.: Mandible and skull segmentation in cone beam computed tomography using supervoxels and graph clustering. Vis. Comput. **35**(10), 1461–1474 (2018). https://doi.org/10.1007/s00371-018-1511-0

13. Ghadimi, S., et al.: Skull segmentation and reconstruction from newborn CT images using coupled level sets. IEEE J. Biomed. Health Inform. **20**(2), 563–573 (2016)
14. Zille, D., et al.: The evolution of surgical planning in orthognathic surgery: EC dental. Science **17**(11), 1914–1919 (2018)
15. Chen, L., et al.: Semantic image segmentation with task-specific edge detection using CNNs and a discriminatively trained domain transform. In: 2016 IEEE Conference on Computer Vision and Pattern Recognition (CVPR) (2016)
16. Lu, F., Wu, F., Hu, P., Peng, Z., Kong, D.: Automatic 3D liver location and segmentation via convolutional neural network and graph cut. Int. J. Comput. Assist. Radiol. Surg. **12**(2), 171–182 (2016). https://doi.org/10.1007/s11548-016-1467-3
17. Cardoso, M.J., et al.: Medical segmentation decathlon. In: Workshop, Medical Image Computing and Computer-Assisted Intervention (MICCAI) (2018)

# Improving the Automatic Cranial Implant Design in Cranioplasty by Linking Different Datasets

Marek Wodzinski[1,2]($\boxtimes$) (ID), Mateusz Daniol[1] (ID), and Daria Hemmerling[1] (ID)

[1] Department of Measurement and Electronics,
AGH University of Science and Technology, Krakow, Poland
wodzinski@agh.edu.pl

[2] Information Systems Institute, University of Applied Sciences Western Switzerland
(HES-SO Valais), Sierre, Switzerland

**Abstract.** The automatic design of cranial implants is an important and challenging task. The implants must be designed according to the individual characterization of the patient's defect. This makes the process tedious and time consuming. However, if possible, the personalized implants should be designed and fabricated during the surgical procedure that requires the implant modeling to be as efficient as possible.

The design of the cranial implants may be improved and accelerated by deep learning-based segmentation networks. This approach transfers the computational burden to the training phase, allowing a real-time inference. Moreover, the practical method should be fully automatic, without the need for manual parameter tuning related to the defect characterization. Therefore, a single, universal model is desirable during practical usage. Nevertheless, deep learning-based solutions require large amount of training data that is difficult to acquire and annotate.

To address this problem, we propose a method to connect the two training sets from the AutoImplant challenge, together with a dedicated U-Net based segmentation network. The datasets are combined by the affine and non-rigid registration, and then are further augmented by random affine transformations. The segmentation method consists of two sequential networks responsible for general structure modelling and the preservation of fine details respectively.

We evaluate the proposed results using test sets for all tasks from the AutoImplant 2021 challenge. Three evaluation metrics are used: Dice Score, Boundary Dice Score, and the 95th percentile of the Hausdorff distance. The method achieves mean Dice Score close to and above 0.9 for Task 1 and 3 respectively. The mean Hausdorff distance is close to 1.5 mm. This shows the method good accuracy and robustness. The qualitative results for Task 2 are unavailable at the moment of writing the manuscript.

**Keywords:** AutoImplant · Deep learning · Cranial implant · Image segmentation · MICCAI challenge

© Springer Nature Switzerland AG 2021
J. Li and J. Egger (Eds.): AutoImplant 2021, LNCS 13123, pp. 29–44, 2021.
https://doi.org/10.1007/978-3-030-92652-6_4

# 1    Introduction

The aim of cranioplasty procedures is to correct the patient's head distortions, as well as to supplement the bone loss, which - for cosmetic reasons and due to the need to provide the required brain protection against further potential damage and mechanical injuries - constitutes a great problem in neurosurgery. Cranioplasty involve lifting the scalp and restoring the skull shape and volume with the original skull piece or implant. Two main conditions must be met for the successful cranioplasty: (i) the proper adjustment of the geometric form of implant, and (ii) the choice of biocompatibile material of the prosthesis supplementing the space after the removed bone flap.

In this work, we address the automatic, fast 3D reconstruction of individually adapted cranial implants that is very desirable in cranioplasty. The aim of the work is the modeling of cranial implants by an automatic, volumetric 3-D shape completion, adapted to the given skull with a defect. As a result, an implant is created that allows the natural maintenance of skull shape to be preserved at the site of the cavity. The first approaches for reconstructing skull bones were done using statistical shape models (SSMs) [6]. Within the development of deep neural networks the paper published in [16] firstly demonstrated a denoising autoencoder to predict a complete skull from defective skull using MRI data with very coarse skulls and simple holes. The further algorithms development included voxel grid completion using CNN networks [4,8], point/mesh completion [21,23], medical images [12,14]. The first challenge for cranial implant design as a shape completion problem was organized as the AutoImplant 2020 challenge [1,12]. The database contained over 200 healthy skulls and each of them had a virtual defect (100 for training, 100 for testing) [12]. Additional 10 skulls with distinct defect shapes, sizes and positions were prepared to evaluate how well the algorithms generalize to varied defects. The goal was to predict the binary implant masks directly from binary skull images (voxel grids) [12]. The shape of the implant to complete the skull can be learnt directly from a defective skull by filling the defected region in defected skull [9–11,15,19] and as the difference between the complete skull and defective skull [3,5,9,13,17,20]. The results from AutoImplant 2020 Challenge are very promising. The highest mean Dice Similarity Coefficient (DSC) for both parts of prepared datasets (100 and 10 cases) was at the level 0.944 and 0.932 respectively implementing U-Net with residual blocks [5]. Other approaches included the usage of SSM + 2D GAN, ED + SE block, Cascade U-Net implementation bringing DSC above 0.9 for both datasets [5,17,20]. The problem to create an automatic algorithm for perfect implant reconstruction is still very challenging and new algorithms are tested and developed, as well as the defect databases include more heterogeneous pathological examples.

In this paper, we present our contribution to the AutoImplant 2021 challenge. The challenge is about volumetric reconstruction of cranial defects. The challenge consists of 3 tasks: the cranial implant design for diverse synthetic defects on aligned skulls (Task 1), cranial implant design for real patient defects (Task 2), improving the model generalisation ability for cranial implant design (Task 3).

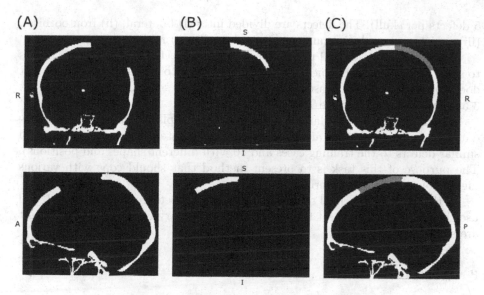

**Fig. 1.** The exemplary visualization of the skull with real defect (A), the automatically designed implant (B), and both the A) and B) overlaid. The visualization presents Case 11 from Task 2 evaluation set.

One of the main goals of the Task 1 is to evaluate the quality of high-resolution fit of the reconstructed shape to the original skull [2]. The Task 2 evaluates the performance of algorithms prepared for automatic implant design translated to various cases with real cranial defects. The representation of a real case from Task 2 with implant design and a skull with a matching implant is shown in Fig. 1. The goal of the Task 3 is to improve the model generalisation ability for cranial implant design [2]. In our work, we decided to use a single model for all the challenge tasks since in practice, the user does not want to care about the alignment of the skull, neither about the defect type.

**Contribution:** In this work, we propose a learning-based method consisting of a single model trained on synthetic defects that successfully generalizes into previously unseen real cranial defects. We develop a method to combine different datasets into a common representation. We evaluate the proposed method on all tasks introduced during the AutoImplant 2021 challenge and show the method accuracy and robustness.

## 2    Dataset

The challenge consists of 3 separate but similar tasks. The Task 1 is about proposing a method being able to model implants for defects with random shapes and positions, however, with roughly aligned skulls. The Task consists of 570 training cases (114 skulls, 5 defects per skull) and 100 testing cases (20 skulls,

5 defects per skull). The defects are divided into: (i) bilateral, (ii) frontoorbital, (iii) parietotemporal, (iv) random (1), and finally (v) random (2) [2].

The Task 2 consists of 11 real patient's cranial defects. The goal of this task is to show the method robustness and generalizbility into real defects. The dataset does not contain training cases. We used the training sets from Task 1 and Task 3 as the training set for the Task 2.

The Task 3 uses the dataset from the AutoImplant 2020 challenge. The database consists of 100 training and 110 testing cases (divided into 100 with similar defects to the training cases and 10 with different shapes and positions). The purpose of this task is to present method that should cope with various high-resolution defect patterns.

In this work, we decided to combine the training sets from Task 1 and 3, and use them as the training set for Task 2. The exemplary cases from each dataset are shown in Fig. 2.

## 3   Methods

### 3.1   Overview

The proposed method is a learning-based procedure. The training phase consists of the following steps: (i) the initial preprocessing, (ii) dataset linking and augmentation, (iii) U-Net-based segmentation. The goal of the first two steps is to connect different datasets into similar representation that can be shared during the training process. Moreover, during the inference additional postprocessing steps are introduced to improve the reconstruction quality and to preserve the input resolution. The inference pipeline is shown in Fig. 3.

### 3.2   Preprocessing

The preprocessing starts with finding the defect boundaries and cropping the image to contain only the defect. This is especially important for Task 1 dataset that strongly suffers from the unused space. An additional offset is introduced to handle cases for which the actual implant may protrude beyond the outline of the actual defected skull. Then, the image is resampled to a given voxel spacing (equal to $1.0 \times 1.0 \times 1.0$ mm in the following experiments). The output spacing is a tuneable parameter, influencing the GPU memory utilization during the training and inference. Finally, the resampled images are padded to the same shape ($222 \times 184 \times 220$ in the performed experiments). The output shape is connected with the voxel spacing and should be tuned accordingly. During the training phase the preprocessing is performed offline.

### 3.3   Dataset Linking and Augmentation

The main goal of the proposed method is to propose an automatic method being able to generalize into unseen, real cases. Therefore, we decided to use

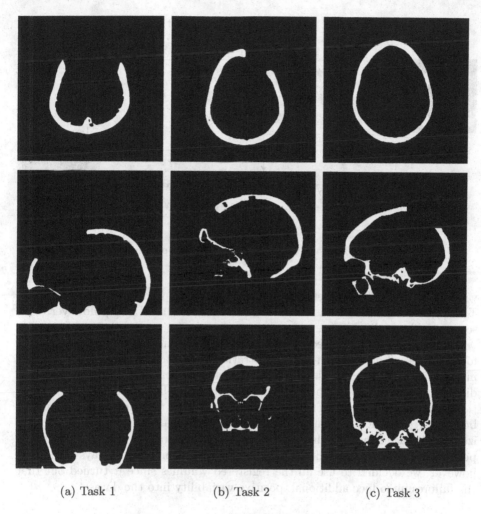

(a) Task 1                (b) Task 2                (c) Task 3

**Fig. 2.** Exemplary cases from Task 1 (a), Task 2 (b), Task 3 (c). Note that the localization of Task 1 cases is different from the remaining ones and a lot of empty, unused space is introduced. Moreover, the initial processing is different.

a single model to all the challenge tasks. This approach, however, requires a way to combine the datasets during training. Thus, after the preprocessing the complete skulls are registered in "all vs all" manner. It means that the complete skulls are first combined into a single dataset and then every skull is registered to all others from both the Task 1 and Task 3. Then, the calculated displacement fields are used to warp the artificial defects (since there are numerous defects per skull for Task 1). This approach resulted in 120 000 training volumes that were further augmented by random flipping and affine transformations. As a result, no overfitting was observed during training. The datasets were divided into training and validation sets before the linking and no registration was performed for the

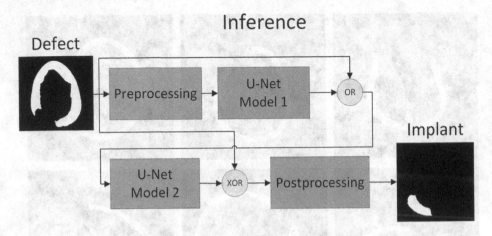

**Fig. 3.** Visualization of the processing pipeline.

validation cases. The dataset linking and registration pipeline is shown in Fig. 4. The registration approach is similar to the one introduced in [5], however, with some significant differences.

The images are registered using a multilevel instance optimization approach for both the affine and non-rigid registration [22]. First, a 3-D affine transformation matrix is calculated. Then, the transformation matrix is converted to a displacement field that is the starting point for the following non-rigid registration. The local normalized cross-correlation is used as the similarity measure for both the registration steps and the diffusive regularization is applied to regularize the displacement field during the non-rigid registration. The registration is performed offline prior to the training. The registration is not always successful, however, we decided to use all the registered volumes since it turned out that the failures introduce additional, positive variability into the dataset.

### 3.4  U-Net-Based Segmentation

The method consists of two networks with the same architecture, however, without weights sharing. The first network is responsible for predicting the cranial implant. Then, the predicted implant is combined with the defect resulting in an imperfect complete skull. This serves as the input for the second network that predicts the complete skull. The exclusive disjunction is then calculated between the input and the output of the second network to predict the final implant. Intuitively, the first network is responsible for generating the general structure of the implant while the second network should recover the fine details and preserve good connection at the boundaries between the implant and the skull.

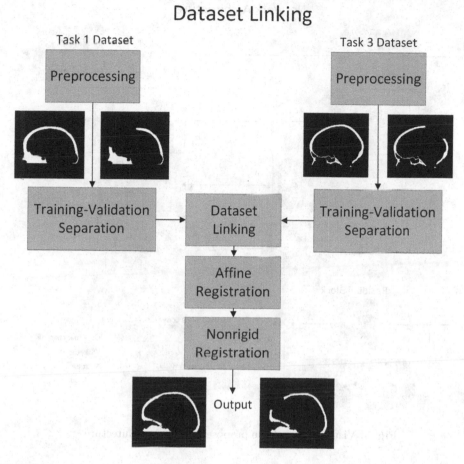

**Fig. 4.** Visualization of combining the Task 1 and 3 datasets into a single training set.

The architecture is a U-Net-based architecture [18] with additional skip connections. The network architecture is shown in Fig. 5. We did not observe any further improvements by making the network deeper and increasing the number of parameters. The network was trained using the soft Dice score as the objective function. The training was performed using 1000 iterations with 500 cases per iteration. The batch case was set to 1. We used Adam optimizer with the initial learning rate equal to 0.002. The learning rate was decreased by a factor of 0.997 after each iteration.

## Network Architecture

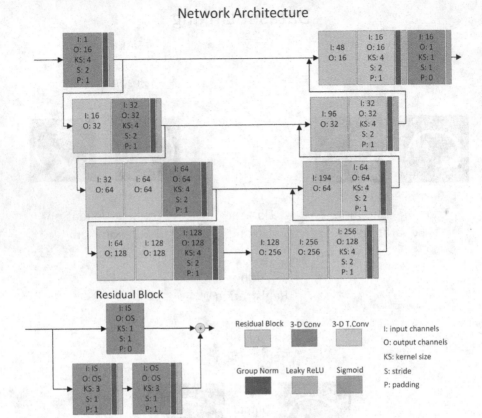

**Fig. 5.** Visualization of the proposed network architecture.

### 3.5 Postprocessing

The postprocessing starts with the conversion of the input images to the original pixel spacing, orientation, and shape. This starts with cropping that reverses the padding introduced during the preprocessing. Then, the image is resampled to the original resolution and zero-padded to reverse the initial boundaries cropping.

Basic operations on binary images are performed to remove small artifacts and to smooth the upsampled implant. This process starts with image labeling to remove noise. Then, the implant is combined with the skull and the binary closing is performed to smooth the boundaries between the implant and the actual defect. This process is performed only within the implant neighbourhood to prevent the process from introducing additional artifacts in different image regions. In case of multiple defects, all of them are processed by checking the connectivity to the skull. Finally, the image is again labeled to remove the final artifacts introduced during the binary closing.

# 4  Results

## 4.1  Overview

The Task 1 and the Task 3 are evaluated using Dice Similarity Score (DSC), 95% Hausdorff distance (HD95) and the boundary DSC (bDSC) [2]. In addition, the Task 2 is being evaluated manually by two experienced neurosurgeons. The quantitative evaluation for Task 2 serves only as an addition because the actual implants differ strongly from the actual defect. The DSC is used to quantify the area overlap between the predicted with the ground truth implant design and shape. The Hausdorff distance measures how far the contours of the predicted implants are from the ground truth. The HD95 is the Hausdorff distance at the 95th percentile. The bDSC is used to measure the possible agreement over predicted and ground truth implant curves.

## 4.2  Task 1

The evaluation set for Task 1 consists of 100 cases. The quantitative results are shown in Table 1. The average DSC value for all the cranial defects is 0.894. Border DSC average value for all the validation cases is 0.934 and HD95 is 1.601. The highest average DSCs and bDSCs were achieved for defects from random_1 set, whereas the standard deviation between different positions of cranial defect for DSC and bDSC values were at the level of 0.010. The lowest values of DSC and bDSC were calculated for frontoorbital defect placement. The highest DSC was calculated for parietotemporal case (equal to 0.948) and the lowest value was calculated for random_2 case (equal to 0.939). The mean HD95 was the highest for bilateral location of the defect and the lowest for the defects located in parietotemporal skull part. The highest value of HD95 represented bilateral location and the lowest value of HD95 parietotemporal defect location. The Fig. 6 shows the DSC results for different locations of the skull's defect for all the evaluation set. Exemplary visualizations of the implant design for each location of the cranial defect are presented in the Fig. 7.

## 4.3  Task 2

The Task 2 consists of 11 real cases with cranial defects. The best evaluation measures were achieved: DSC value for case 11, the bDSC value for case 6 and the HD95 value belongs to case 3. On the other hand, the lowest quality measures were calculated as follows: DSC and dDSC for case 3, and HD95 for case 11. Based on the quantitative results (Table 2), the best implant design was achieved for case 11, whereas the worst match was calculated for case 03. The visual comparison of both results are shown in Fig. 8. It is seen that in the worst case, the algorithm also designed other parts in skull shape (red dots located all around the skull), however this should not influence the qualitative evaluation. The mean DSC value for all the cases was 0.524, the bDSC is 0.482, the HD95 is 54.516. The qualitative results are not available at the moment of writing the

**Table 1.** The quantitative results for the Task 1 test set using the DSC, bDSC and HD95.

| | | Bilateral | Frontoorbital | Parietotemporal | Random_1 | Random_2 | Overall |
|---|---|---|---|---|---|---|---|
| DSC | Average | 0.885 | 0.880 | 0.906 | 0.907 | 0.893 | 0.894 |
| | Min | 0.704 | 0.841 | 0.767 | 0.862 | 0.636 | 0.636 |
| | Max | 0.947 | 0.937 | 0.948 | 0.946 | 0.939 | 0.948 |
| | Std | 0.056 | 0.025 | 0.045 | 0.022 | 0.067 | 0.020 |
| bDSC | Average | 0.937 | 0.915 | 0.942 | 0.937 | 0.938 | 0.934 |
| | Min | 0.877 | 0.870 | 0.874 | 0.906 | 0.901 | 0.870 |
| | Max | 0.966 | 0.953 | 0.963 | 0.954 | 0.960 | 0.966 |
| | Std | 0.020 | 0.019 | 0.019 | 0.013 | 0.015 | 0.003 |
| HD95 [mm] | Average | 2.049 | 1.536 | 1.303 | 1.531 | 1.584 | 1.601 |
| | Min | 0.980 | 1.131 | 0.800 | 0.894 | 0.894 | 0.800 |
| | Max | 5.154 | 2.154 | 2.561 | 2.400 | 4.932 | 5.154 |
| | Std | 0.973 | 0.286 | 0.471 | 0.437 | 0.868 | 0.305 |

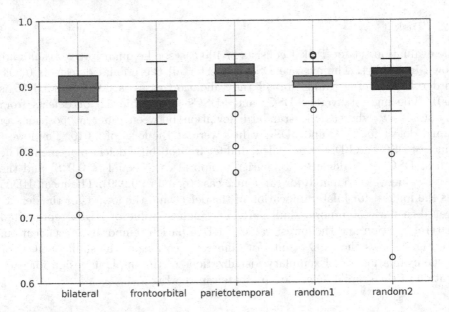

**Fig. 6.** The DSC results for each testing case for different location of cranial defects (Task 1).

manuscript. Importantly, the quantitative results should be treated with care because they are based on a comparison with the real implants that are much thinner than the actual defect.

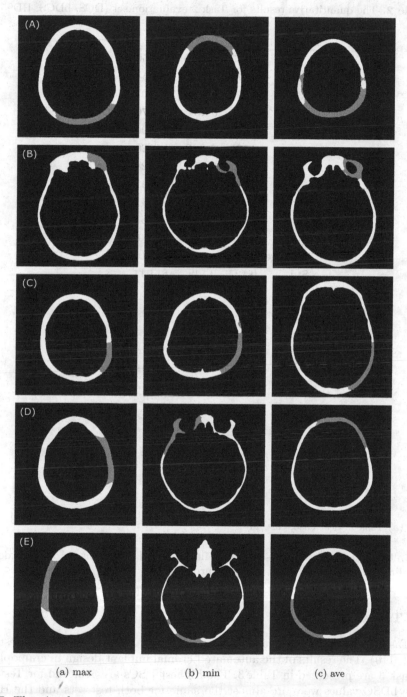

(a) max                    (b) min                    (c) ave

**Fig. 7.** The visual comparison of implant design for bilateral (A), frontoorbital (B), parietotemporal (C), random_1 (D), random_2 (E) cranial defects (Task 1).

**Table 2.** The quantitative results for Task 2 evaluation set (DCS, bDCS, HD95).

| ID | DSC | bDSC | HD95 [mm] |
|---|---|---|---|
| 1 | 0.485 | 0.515 | 7.550 |
| 2 | 0.576 | 0.514 | 185.154 |
| 3 | 0.259 | 0.170 | 215.607 |
| 4 | 0.511 | 0.478 | 10.770 |
| 5 | 0.570 | 0.543 | 7.000 |
| 6 | 0.535 | **0.668** | 14.526 |
| 7 | 0.402 | 0.374 | 12.728 |
| 8 | 0.446 | 0.323 | 130.041 |
| 9 | 0.682 | 0.474 | 7.141 |
| 10 | 0.595 | 0.582 | 6.164 |
| 11 | **0.705** | 0.666 | **3.000** |
| Average | 0.524 | 0.482 | 54.516 |
| Std | 0.127 | 0.148 | 81.043 |

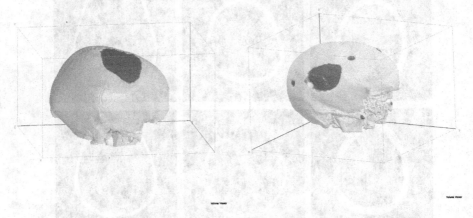

(a) Task 2: best case, case 11              (b) Task 2: worst case, case 03

**Fig. 8.** The 3-D visual comparison of best fit (a) and the worst fit (b) implant design for real cranial defects (Task 2). (Color figure online)

## 4.4    Task 3

The Task 3 consists of two evaluation sets: Test Set 1 (case 1–100) and Test Set 2 (101–110). The results of the automated cranial implant design in cranioplasty for Task 3 are presented in Table 3. The highest DSCs are achieved for Test Set 1, the bDSC values were are almost the same for both test sets and the HD95 was lower for Test Set 1. The overall performance of this task designates the DSC average value at the level of 0.933, the bDSC average values equal to 0.953

and HD95 to 1.478. The results between both Test Sets are very similar (the DSC average value differs only of 0.008), The HD95 differs between both test sets of 0.022.

**Table 3.** The quantitative results for Task 3 for cases 1–100 (Test Set 1), 101–110 (Test Set 2), and the overall results (DSC, bDSC and HD95).

|          |         | Test Set 1 | Test Set 2 | Overall |
|----------|---------|------------|------------|---------|
| DSC      | Average | 0.934      | 0.926      | 0.933   |
|          | Min     | 0.768      | 0.872      | 0.768   |
|          | Max     | 0.961      | 0.952      | 0.961   |
|          | Std     | 0.024      | 0.025      | 0.024   |
| bDSC     | Average | 0.953      | 0.953      | 0.953   |
|          | Min     | 0.715      | 0.939      | 0.715   |
|          | Max     | 0.974      | 0.961      | 0.974   |
|          | Std     | 0.027      | 0.006      | 0.025   |
| HD95 [mm]| Average | 1.476      | 1.498      | 1.478   |
|          | Min     | 0.778      | 0.646      | 0.646   |
|          | Max     | 19.420     | 3.125      | 19.420  |
|          | Std     | 1.852      | 0.744      | 1.780   |

## 5    Discussion and Conclusion

The achieved results confirm the proposed method accuracy and robustness. There are not any significant outliers. The reconstructions seem reasonable from both the qualitative and quantitative perspectives. There are some minor errors (e.g. for a few huge frontal defects the eye orbits are considered as the defects because they are connected with the actual defect), however, these cases are usually not realistic and, moreover, further work should eliminate these issues. In Task 1, the results are similar for all the defect types with the highest variability within the bilateral defects. For a few synthetic cases with extremely large defects the DSC is significantly smaller than the bDSC, however, this should be expected since there are many possible reconstructions for cases with unavailable symmetry, and the behavior deep within the defect is undefined.

The proposed method is similar to the winner from the first edition of the challenge. We use a similar architecture and the image registration to augment the training set. However, there are two main differences. The first one is connected with the datasets linking by the image registration instead of only augmenting the training set for a given task. Moreover, we used different image registration algorithm and accepted failures. Another difference is connected with the architecture. We used two-step procedure to improve the recovery of fine details. This resulted in minor improvements in the DSC or bDSC (about 0.01), however, the mean HD95 decreased by about 0.5 mm that is a considerable improvement.

Our method uses a single model for all the tasks, however, we are aware that the quantitative test results would be better using a separate models. For example, our initial tests have shown that it is possible to achieve bDSC close to 0.96 for Task 1 alone with the preprocessing limited to a simple resampling, without alternating the defect positions. Nevertheless, such an approach is not practical because it would enforce the end-user to have the knowledge about the characterization of the given models. Even more importantly, this approach does not generalize well into slightly different problems and even the initial preprocessing strongly influences the final results. Thus, these models would be useless for the Task 2 dataset for which our method generalizes relatively well.

The quantitative results for Task 2 (Table 2) at the first glance may seem to be much worse than for the remaining tasks (Table 1 and Table 3). However, it should be noted that the quantitative results for Task 2 were calculated with respect to the actual implant, not the reconstructed defects as in the Task 1 and 3. Therefore, the quantitative results are not that representative and should be interpreted with care. Unfortunately, the qualitative results are not available at the moment of writing this manuscript. Some of the calculated implants for Task 2 contain additional, small artifacts. This significantly increases the HD95, however, it does not influence the qualitative results and the usability.

This brings the discussion to another point - the practical use of the reconstructed defects. A lot of them are not implantable in practice due to their geometry and position. Therefore, the defects should be accompanied by another method describing how the implants should be divided prior to the surgical procedure together with the detailed and sequential plan of their implantation. The development of such a method should be possible using the reinforcement learning. This, together with a correctly positioned visualization in augmented reality would result in a great, practical tool [7].

Another topic that requires further investigation is the dataset augmentation. We plan to extended the proposed method with GAN-based synthesis of additional synthetic skulls and defects. Even though our training set is huge (120 000 volumes further augmented by affine transformations), the information within it is limited because it was created from only 214 skulls with synthetic defects. We hope that additional data synthesis using GANs will enable even better generalizability of the proposed method. After the mentioned improvements, we plan to make the source code publicly available.

To conclude, we proposed a deep learning-based method to automatically model the personalized cranial implants. We combined different training sets from the AutoImplant 2021 challenge by an appropriate preprocessing followed by the nonrigid registration and then augmented it further with random affine transformations. The approach resulted in a single model being able to accurately reconstruct the synthetic defects with various shapes and sizes. Moreover, the proposed method was able to generalize the learned knowledge into unseen test cases containing the real defects.

**Acknowledgments.** This research was supported in part by PLGrid Infrastructure and the by the Ministry of Science and Higher Education in Poland, statutory activity of AGH UST.

# References

1. AutoImplant Grand Challange 2020 (2020). https://autoimplant.grand-challenge. org/. Accessed 16 Sept 2021
2. AutoImplant Grand Challange 2021 (2021). https://autoimplant2021.grand-challenge.org/. Accessed 18 Sept 2021
3. Bayat, A., Shit, S., Kilian, A., Liechtenstein, J.T., Kirschke, J.S., Menze, B.H.: Cranial implant prediction using low-resolution 3D shape completion and high-resolution 2D refinement. In: Li, J., Egger, J. (eds.) AutoImplant 2020. LNCS, vol. 12439, pp. 77–84. Springer, Cham (2020). https://doi.org/10.1007/978-3-030-64327-0_9
4. Dai, A., Ruizhongtai Qi, C., Nießner, M.: Shape completion using 3D-encoder-predictor CNNS and shape synthesis. In: Proceedings of the IEEE Conference on Computer Vision and Pattern Recognition, pp. 5868–5877 (2017)
5. Ellis, D.G., Aizenberg, M.R.: Deep learning using augmentation via registration: 1st place solution to the AutoImplant 2020 challenge. In: Li, J., Egger, J. (eds.) AutoImplant 2020. LNCS, vol. 12439, pp. 47–55. Springer, Cham (2020). https://doi.org/10.1007/978-3-030-64327-0_6
6. Fuessinger, M.A.: Planning of skull reconstruction based on a statistical shape model combined with geometric morphometrics. Int. J. Comput. Assist. Radiol. Surg. **13**(4), 519–529 (2018)
7. Gsaxner, C., Eck, U., Schmalstieg, D., Navab, N., Egger, J.: Augmented reality in oral and maxillofacial surgery. In: Computer-Aided Oral and Maxillofacial Surgery, pp. 107–139 (2021)
8. Han, X., Li, Z., Huang, H., Kalogerakis, E., Yu, Y.: High-resolution shape completion using deep neural networks for global structure and local geometry inference. In: Proceedings of the IEEE International Conference on Computer Vision, pp. 85–93 (2017)
9. Jin, Y., Li, J., Egger, J.: High-resolution cranial implant prediction via patch-wise training. In: Li, J., Egger, J. (eds.) AutoImplant 2020. LNCS, vol. 12439, pp. 94–103. Springer, Cham (2020). https://doi.org/10.1007/978-3-030-64327-0_11
10. Kodym, O., Španěl, M., Herout, A.: Cranial defect reconstruction using cascaded CNN with alignment. In: Li, J., Egger, J. (eds.) AutoImplant 2020. LNCS, vol. 12439, pp. 56–64. Springer, Cham (2020). https://doi.org/10.1007/978-3-030-64327-0_7
11. Li, J., Pepe, A., Gsaxner, C., Campe, G., Egger, J., et al.: A baseline approach for AutoImplant: the MICCAI 2020 cranial implant design challenge. In: Erdt, M. (ed.) CLIP/ML-CDS -2020. LNCS, vol. 12445, pp. 75–84. Springer, Cham (2020). https://doi.org/10.1007/978-3-030-60946-7_8
12. Li, J., et al.: AutoImplant 2020-first MICCAI challenge on automatic cranial implant design. IEEE Trans. Med. Imag. (2021)

13. Mainprize, J.G., Fishman, Z., Hardisty, M.R.: Shape completion by U-Net: an approach to the AutoImplant MICCAI cranial implant design challenge. In: Li, J., Egger, J. (eds.) AutoImplant 2020. LNCS, vol. 12439, pp. 65–76. Springer, Cham (2020). https://doi.org/10.1007/978-3-030-64327-0_8

14. Manjón, J.V., et al.: Blind MRI brain lesion inpainting using deep learning. In: Burgos, N., Svoboda, D., Wolterink, J.M., Zhao, C. (eds.) SASHIMI 2020. LNCS, vol. 12417, pp. 41–49. Springer, Cham (2020). https://doi.org/10.1007/978-3-030-59520-3_5

15. Matzkin, F., Newcombe, V., Glocker, B., Ferrante, E.: Cranial implant design via virtual craniectomy with shape priors. In: Li, J., Egger, J. (eds.) AutoImplant 2020. LNCS, vol. 12439, pp. 37–46. Springer, Cham (2020). https://doi.org/10.1007/978-3-030-64327-0_5

16. Morais, A., Egger, J., Alves, V.: Automated computer-aided design of cranial implants using a deep volumetric convolutional denoising autoencoder. In: Rocha, Á., Adeli, H., Reis, L.P., Costanzo, S. (eds.) WorldCIST'19 2019. AISC, vol. 932, pp. 151–160. Springer, Cham (2019). https://doi.org/10.1007/978-3-030-16187-3_15

17. Pimentel, P., et al.: Automated virtual reconstruction of large skull defects using statistical shape models and generative adversarial networks. In: Li, J., Egger, J. (eds.) AutoImplant 2020. LNCS, vol. 12439, pp. 16–27. Springer, Cham (2020). https://doi.org/10.1007/978-3-030-64327-0_3

18. Ronneberger, O., Fischer, P., Brox, T.: U-Net: convolutional networks for biomedical image segmentation. In: Navab, N., Hornegger, J., Wells, W.M., Frangi, A.F. (eds.) MICCAI 2015. LNCS, vol. 9351, pp. 234–241. Springer, Cham (2015). https://doi.org/10.1007/978-3-319-24574-4_28

19. Shi, H., Chen, X.: Cranial implant design through multiaxial slice inpainting using deep learning. In: Li, J., Egger, J. (eds.) AutoImplant 2020. LNCS, vol. 12439, pp. 28–36. Springer, Cham (2020). https://doi.org/10.1007/978-3-030-64327-0_4

20. Wang, B., et al.: Cranial implant design using a deep learning method with anatomical regularization. In: Li, J., Egger, J. (eds.) AutoImplant 2020. LNCS, vol. 12439, pp. 85–93. Springer, Cham (2020). https://doi.org/10.1007/978-3-030-64327-0_10

21. Wen, X., Li, T., Han, Z., Liu, Y.S.: Point cloud completion by skip-attention network with hierarchical folding. In: Proceedings of the IEEE/CVF Conference on Computer Vision and Pattern Recognition, pp. 1939–1948 (2020)

22. Wodzinski, M., Ciepiela, I., Kuszewski, T., Kedzierawski, P., Skalski, A.: Semi-supervised deep learning-based image registration method with volume penalty for real-time breast tumor bed localization. Sensors 21(12), 1–14 (2021)

23. Yuan, W., Khot, T., Held, D., Mertz, C., Hebert, M.: PCN: point completion network. In: 2018 International Conference on 3D Vision (3DV), pp. 728–737. IEEE (2018)

# Learning to Rearrange Voxels in Binary Segmentation Masks for Smooth Manifold Triangulation

Jianning Li[1,2,3,4]($\boxtimes$), Antonio Pepe[1,2], Christina Gsaxner[1,2], Yuan Jin[1,2,5], and Jan Egger[1,2,4]

[1] Institute of Computer Graphics and Vision, Graz University of Technology, Inffeldgasse 16, 8010 Graz, Austria
{jianning.li,egger}@icg.tugraz.at
[2] Computer Algorithms for Medicine Laboratory (Café-Lab), 8010 Graz, Austria
[3] Research Unit Experimental Neurotraumatology, Department of Neurosurgery, Medical University Graz, Auenbruggerplatz 2², 8036 Graz, Austria
[4] Institute for AI in Medicine (IKIM), University Hospital Essen, Girardetstraße 2, 45131 Essen, Germany
[5] Research Center for Connected Healthcare Big Data, Zhejiang Lab, Hangzhou 311121, Zhejiang, China

**Abstract.** Medical images, especially volumetric images, are of high resolution and often exceed the capacity of standard desktop GPUs. As a result, most deep learning-based medical image analysis tasks require the input images to be downsampled, often substantially, before these can be fed to a neural network. However, downsampling can lead to a loss of image quality, which is undesirable especially in reconstruction tasks, where the fine geometric details need to be preserved. In this paper, we propose that high-resolution images can be reconstructed in a coarse-to-fine fashion, where a deep learning algorithm is only responsible for generating a coarse representation of the image, which consumes moderate GPU memory. For producing the high-resolution outcome, we propose two novel methods: learned voxel rearrangement of the coarse output and hierarchical image synthesis. Compared to the coarse output, the high-resolution counterpart allows for smooth surface triangulation, which can be 3D-printed in the highest possible quality. Experiments of this paper are carried out on the dataset of AutoImplant 2021 (https://autoimplant2021.grand-challenge.org/), a MICCAI challenge on cranial implant design. The dataset contains high-resolution skulls that can be viewed as 2D manifolds embedded in a 3D space. Codes associated with this study can be accessed at https://github.com/Jianningli/voxel_rearrangement.

**Keywords:** Skull reconstruction · Cranial implant design · Deep learning · Manifold · Sparse CNN · Nearest neighbor search (NNS) · Hash table · Super resolution · Hamming distance · 3D printing

© Springer Nature Switzerland AG 2021
J. Li and J. Egger (Eds.): AutoImplant 2021, LNCS 13123, pp. 45–62, 2021.
https://doi.org/10.1007/978-3-030-92652-6_5

# 1   Introduction

## 1.1   Background

For many medical image analysis tasks, the high-resolution images, especially 3D images, have to be downsampled before they can be fed into deep neural networks, due to limited GPU capacity. However, downsampling can often lead to severe degradation of image quality and loss of subtle structures, which is unacceptable, especially in precision-demanding reconstruction tasks.

## 1.2   Related Work

In tackling the problem of high memory consumption of large 3D medical images, the medical image analysis community has come up with several techniques, which we roughly grouped into three categories based on which part of the image analysis pipeline these techniques have targeted: the medical image itself, the network architecture or the data structure.

**Medical Images.** Dividing the high-resolution medical images into smaller patches is the most intuitive and prevalently adopted method to fit the image to the available GPU memory. If necessary, the strategies of cropping patches from an image have to be adapted to the characteristics of the data. For example, Li, J. et al. [10] proposed to train a deep neural network using successive non-overlapping patches and overlapping patches, so that the network can learn the global shape distribution of the high-resolution, spatially sparse skull data effectively. Akil, M. et al. [1] extracted overlapping patches from MRI images for brain tumor segmentation, considering that using overlapping patches cropped from the images helps the deep neural network to learn the spatial relationship among patches.

Other researchers have investigated detail-preserving image downsampling techniques [4], which allow for the reduction of image size without substantially degrading the image quality.

**Network Architecture.** Two popular network structures dealing with high-resolution medical images include the *coarse-to-fine* framework and the cascaded neural network. As the name suggests, under the *coarse-to-fine* framework, a network first produces a coarse image output, which is further refined to approximate the ground truth. In [12], the authors first trained an autoencoer on downsampled skull images. The corresponding coarse output is used to extract the region of interest (ROI) of the original high-resolution defective skull. The size of the ROI, compared to the whole image, is reduced substantially, while no details essential to the specific task have been discarded. The ROI is then used to train another autoencoder to produce the final fine output. In [7], in order to perform shape completion on high-resolution ($256^3$) grids, the authors first trained a neural network on the coarse counterpart of the object ($32^3$), which, even if is of low resolution, contains the global shape information of an object. The corresponding learnt feature maps are used to guide the training of another neural network, which works on patches cropped along the missing region of the original high-resolution object ($256^3$). The work of Dai, A. et al. [3] is the closest to our study, in which the coarse output of the first network is hierarchically synthesized to higher resolution, based on an image template.

Kodym, O. et al. [8,9] used cascaded convolutional neural networks (CNN) for skull shape completion, where the first network (3D U-net) takes as input downsampled skull volumes ($64^3$) and produces a coarse output. The second network takes as input the preceding output (upsampled to $128^3$) as well as an equally sized patch cropped from the original high-resolution skull and produces the final high-resolution output.

**Data Structure.** Some medical images (e.g., the skull) have unique characteristics such that a memory-efficient data structure can be tailor-made for them. Graham, B. et al. have devised *Submanifold Sparse CNN* [5,6], a set of convolutional operations tailored for processing spatially sparse data in the form of submanifolds. Different from conventional convolutional filters that slide over the entire image space, including the object of interest and the background, sparse convolutions run only on the object. This is efficient, memory-saving and requires substantially fewer floating point operations (FLOPs), especially when the object occupies only a small percentage of the entire volume (like the skull, which is essentially a two-dimensional surface in a 3D volumetric space, i.e., a manifold). Similarly, Riegler, G. et al. and Wang, P. et al. [14,15] devised octree-based CNN, which can learn shape representations from high-resolution data stored in an octree data structure.

## 2   Dataset

The datasets for *Task 3* of the AutoImplant 2021 challenge (https://auto implant2021.grand-challenge.org/) were used. They account for 100 triplets of complete skulls, artificial defective skulls and the corresponding implants for training and 110 triplets for testing[1]. According to [11], the skulls are binary segmentation masks with a very low voxel occupancy rate (VOR, usually less than 10%), indicating that in the large volumetric space, $512 \times 512 \times Z$, only a fraction of the voxels contain valid geometric information of the skulls. Existent deep learning-based methods usually take as input the entire volume, which consumes an excessive amount of memory and computation power [13]. Besides sparsity, another characteristic of the skull voxels is that they are distributed approximately spherically (see Fig. 8 in [12] as an example) in the volumetric space, where the non-zero voxels constitute the surface of the skull, making the skull resemble a manifold, topologically.

---

[1] The test set is further split into $D_{100}$, which contains 100 defective skulls with similar defect shapes to those of the training set and $D_{10}$, which includes 10 defective skulls with varied defect patterns.

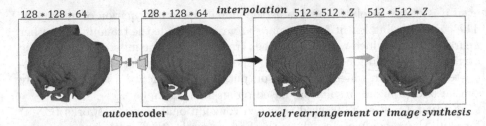

**Fig. 1.** Pipeline of the proposed coarse-to-fine framework for the high-resolution skull shape completion task.

## 3    Method

An extensive review of the solutions presented at the AutoImplant challenge [13] in 2020 has identified two major difficulties of the deep learning-based cranial implant design task: **1)** The skull volumes are of high resolution and a large amount of memory and computation power is needed to process them, taking into consideration of the output of all the intermediate layers. With limited computation resources (especially within clinical settings [2]), the skulls have to be downsampled and, subsequently, the output of networks is coarse. **2)** In high resolution, deep learning models tend not to generalize well across varied defect patterns.

According to one of our earlier works [12] (Appendix A and B), a simple autoencoder shows good generalization performance for shape completion of varied defect patterns when trained on low-resolution (downsampled) skulls, without an augmented training set (only the original 100 skull pairs in the training set provided by the AutoImplant challenge were used). Based on these findings, we propose a coarse-to-fine framework, as illustrated in Fig. 1, where the skull shape completion is carried out on downsampled skulls ($128 \times 128 \times 64$) using an autoencoder network. We use the same autoencoder as the skull shape completion network used in [12], i.e., $N_1$. The low-resolution output is then upsampled to its original resolution, $512 \times 512 \times Z$, using spline interpolation. This results in a coarse upsampled skull, as shown in Fig. 1. As a final step, the geometric details and smoothness of the skull surface is restored through either voxel rearrangement or image synthesis. A detailed description of voxel rearrangement and image synthesis follows.

### 3.1    Learning Voxel Rearrangement

In this study, it is assumed that, through rearrangement of the empty and non-empty voxels, the surface of a coarse skull can be smoothed and the geometric details can be restored. It should be noted that the surface smoothness obtained via voxel rearrangement substantially differs from that obtained using smoothing filters such as median or Gaussian filters, which are not detail-preserving filters. Figure 2 shows an illustration of the (inner and outer) surfaces of a coarse skull

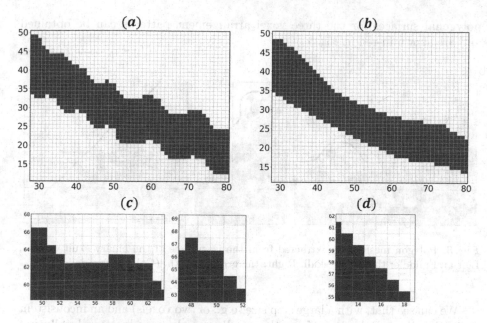

**Fig. 2.** Illustration of voxel arrangement on the surface of coarse (a) and ground truth (b) skulls. (c) and (d) show the dominant voxel arrangement patterns on the two types of skulls.

(a) and the ground truth skull (b), from which we can see the difference of the voxel arrangements between the two. For ease of illustration, we used a 2D grid to represent the volumetric data, where the filled grid cells stand for occupied voxels (valued 1) and the blank cells stand for background (valued 0). Figure 2(c) and (d) show, respectively, the dominant voxel arrangement patterns on the surface of the coarse skull and the ground truth skull. We can see that, for the ground truth skull in (d), the neighboring occupied voxels tend to be arranged in descending terraces and the step size is only one voxel. Besides, when seeing the occupied voxels in the grid as a curve, the sign of the first derivative is consistent. In comparison, the step size for the occupied voxels on the coarse skull is usually larger, e.g., two voxels, and the derivative sign can change locally.

Different voxel arrangement patterns can result in different triangulation results on the binary masks, as illustrated in Fig. 3, where the occupied voxels are depicted using blue dots on the vertices of the 2D grid. Taking the marching cubes algorithm as example, which extracts a polygon mesh from the isosurface (the skull surface formed by all the occupied voxels), whether or not an edge of the mesh passes through a cube on the grid is determined by whether there is one edge of the cube that contains two opposite (zero and one) vertices. As previously mentioned, if one vertex of the cube on the grid is one, the vertex belongs to the object and vice versa. Based on this rule, (a segment of) the polygonal surfaces for the three voxel arrangement patterns can be obtained and are shown in red in Fig. 3.

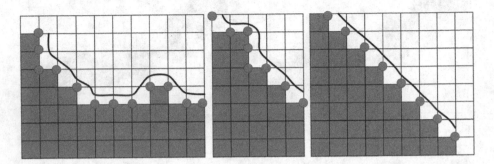

**Fig. 3.** Polygon mesh (red) extracted from the isosurface of the binary skull volume. Left and middle: the coarse skull. Right: the ground truth. (Color figure online)

We can see that, with a large step size (e.g., of two voxels) and an inconsistent derivative sign of the isosurface, the resultant polygon edges are locally not smooth (e.g., they have bumps or '*sharp*' turns). In contrast, the polygon from the ground truth is smooth (Fig. 3, right). It is easy to extend the above concept to 3D, where a skull volume is represented by a 3D grid containing $512 \times 512 \times Z$ cubes.

In our study, we propose to learn a transformation $\mathbf{F}$ from a coarse voxel arrangement (Fig. 2(a)) to a smooth arrangement (Fig. 2(b)), using an autoencoder network. The same autoencoder used for low-resolution skull shape completion is used for the voxel rearrangement, where the input is the the upsampled coarse skull and the ground truth is the original complete skull ($512 \times 512 \times Z$). For each training epoch, $128 \times 128 \times 64$ patches are randomly cropped from the two types of skulls. During inference, as the number of slices $Z$ of each skull differs, we first sequentially feed the upper $\frac{512}{128} \times \frac{512}{128} \times (Z//64)$ patches ($//$ operator takes only the integer after a division) of the image into the trained network. Then, the patches are cropped from the lower 64 slices. The final result is obtained by stitching the output patches in the same sequence as they are fed into the network together. Doing so allows us to handle varied-sized skull volumes.

As both the input and ground truth are binary, learning voxel rearrangement (rearranging the positions of empty and non-empty voxels) can also be viewed as learning a conversion between 0 and 1:

$$\begin{cases} \mathbf{F}(0) = 1 & \text{if } \chi_1 \\ \mathbf{F}(0) = 0 & \text{if } \chi_2 \\ \mathbf{F}(1) = 1 & \text{if } \chi_3 \\ \mathbf{F}(1) = 0 & \text{if } \chi_4 \end{cases} \tag{1}$$

The network learns a set of *rules* $\chi_1, \chi_2, \chi_3, \chi_4$ in order to determine which conversion described in Eq. 1 will be executed during the inference for each voxel position. We cannot describe here precisely what *rules* the network has learnt due to the black box nature of CNN. However, it is safe to assume that the network has to rearrange the voxels based on Fig. 2(a) $\rightarrow$ (b), in order to produce the desired smooth output.

## 3.2   Hierarchical Image Synthesis

Besides using a neural network to learn a smooth voxel arrangement as described in Sect. 3.1, the voxels in a coarse skull can also be updated according to a pre-selected smooth skull template. In this section, we introduce a scheme where the coarse skull output (from the skull shape completion autoencoder trained on downsampled skull data) can be hierarchically synthesized to high resolution, as illustrated in Fig. 4(a). For a fast and memory-efficient synthesis, a tailored hash table-based approximate nearest neighbor search (NNS) strategy and binary encoding is used (Fig. 4(b)). To further speed up the process, we divide each skull into four sub-volumes and the synthesis of each sub-volume is parallelized by making use of the multicore processing potential of the CPU (Fig. 4(c)).

**Hierarchical Image Synthesis.** As shown in Fig. 4(a), Gaussian image pyramids are created for the coarse network output[2], and a randomly selected complete skull from the training set, which will serve as a smooth template. Starting from the bottom pyramid level $L_0$, each voxel in the first ($L_1$, $256 \times 256 \times 128$) and second level ($L_2$, $512 \times 512 \times 256$) of the coarse output image pyramid is replaced by its most similar voxel in the corresponding level of the smooth template image pyramid. The similarity between two voxels, $V1$ and $V2$, is measured by the Hamming distance between the neighbors of the voxels:

$$d_{HM}(V1, V2) = \sum (V1_n \bigoplus V2_n) \tag{2}$$

$V1_n$ and $V2_n$ are the $3^3$ or $5^3$ neighbors of the two voxels. Here, a $3^3$ neighborhood is used. Considering that the images are binary, we used a bit representation of the voxels and their neighbors. For example, the $3^3$ neighborhood of a voxel is stored as a 27-bit long string such as '*ob111001011100...*'. This reduces the memory consumption substantially compared to using the original data type, where each voxel occupies 64 (*int64*) or 32 (*int32*) bits of memory. $\bigoplus$ stands for the bit-wise XOR of the two bit strings. $\sum$ counts the number of non-empty bits.

---

[2] The coarse output (size: $128 \times 128 \times 64$) by the shape completion autoencoder network shown in Fig. 1.

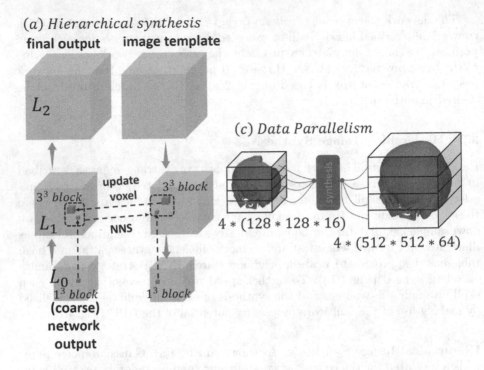

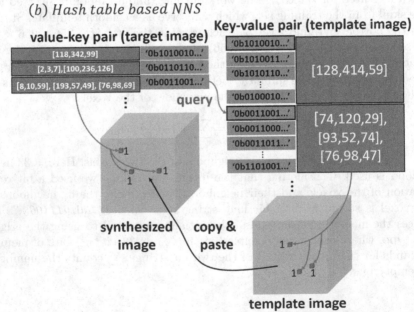

**Fig. 4.** Illustration of voxel updating based on a hierarchical image synthesis pipeline, which consists of three main components: (a) the creation of a hierarchical pyramid, (b) the creation of hash tables and binary encoding, and (c) data parallelism.

**Sparsity and Approximate NNS.** To upsample a coarse skull to a higher resolution, all the voxels in the coarse pyramid have to be updated based on their similarity to the voxels in the template pyramid, which can be formulated as a nearest neighbor search problem. However, using a linear search strategy is impractical in the situation, considering that the number of voxels in a skull volume is usually large, e.g., there are over 60 million voxels in a $512 \times 512 \times 256$ volume. To reduce the required number of searches, we take the sparsity of the skull volume into consideration. For both, the coarse pyramid and the template pyramid, only the voxels whose neighbors are non-empty are involved in the NNS[3]. In other words, we only update the voxels in and around the skull surface.

Similar to the implementation of sparse convolutional operations described in [5,6], we use a hash table to store the bit strings (i.e., the voxels and neighbors) and the corresponding coordinates $(x, y, z)$ for both the coarse pyramid and the template pyramid, as shown in Fig. 4(b). It should be noted that one bit string (the *key* in the hash table) could correspond to multiple coordinates, when several voxels have the same neighbors. In such cases, only a one-time search is required for these voxels, which further reduces the overall number of searches needed.

No matter how large a hash table is, the time complexity of retrieving an entry from a hash table is always $O(1)$, which is a highly desirable property for our task, provided that an entry from the coarse pyramid exists also in the template pyramid (i.e., the Hamming distance is zero). In order to increase the likelihood that a bit string exists in both hash tables, we pre-compute all the bit strings that have an Hamming distance (calculated according to Eq. 2) below three from each actual *key* in the template pyramid. These string neighbors correspond to the same coordinate as the actual *key* that exists in the template pyramid. Experimentally, a set of such neighbors[4] together with the actual keys would guarantee that one entry from the coarse pyramid exists also in the template pyramid with a probability of over 80%. For the remaining voxels, zero and one can be randomly assigned.

Define the sets of actual keys and their neighbors from the template image as $S_{ta} = \{K1_{actual}, K2_{actual}, K3_{actual} \cdots \}$ and $S_{tn} = \{K_{n1}, K_{n2}, K_{n3} \cdots \}$, given a *key* $K_c$ from the coarse pyramid, the coordinates of the voxels in the template pyramid to be used to replace the voxels in the coarse pyramid can be obtained according to Algorithm 1. The process is extremely fast in runtime, even for large hash tables, as the time complexity of the two main operations (i.e., get_value) is constant $O(1)$.

**Data Parallelism.** By making use of the multicore processing potential of the CPU, each skull volume can be divided into four equal patches and the synthesis

---

[3] For example, in a typical $512 \times 512 \times 256$ volume containing the skull, there may only be around three million of such voxels, which is, however, still impractical for a linear search, as over three million $\times$ three million comparisons are needed to update all voxels.

[4] Not to be confused with the $3^3$ and $5^3$ voxel neighbors in the image pyramid.

---

**Algorithm 1:** Retrieving the coordinates corresponding to an entry (bit string) from a hash table

---

**Input:** a *key* $K_c$ from the coarse pyramid ;
**Output:** coordinate(s) $(x, y, z)$ from the template pyramid ;
**if** $K_c$ in $S_{ta}$ **then**
|    coordinates=$S_{ta}$.get_value($K_c$) ;
**else if** $K_c$ in $S_{tn}$ **then**
|    coordinates=$S_{tn}$.get_value($K_c$) ;
**else**
|    assign 0 or 1 to the voxels ;

---

of the patches can be parallelized, as illustrated in Fig. 4(c). Note that if data parallelism is used, the hash tables should also be created for patches, instead of on the whole skull volume. The final output is the combination of the four output synthesized patches.

## 4   Experiment and Results

As described in Sect. 3, an autoencoder is first trained on downsampled skulls ($128 \times 128 \times 64$) for skull shape completion. We evaluate three approaches for upsampling the coarse output to the original resolution ($512 \times 512 \times Z$): spline interpolation, voxel rearrangement (proposed) and hierarchical image synthesis (proposed).

For the interpolation-based upsampling, the completed, coarse skulls produced by the trained shape completion network are upsampled to their original size of $512 \times 512 \times Z$ using spline interpolation.

For the proposed voxel rearrangement-based method, the trained autoencoder runs first on the defective skulls in both the training and test set to produce the corresponding completed and coarse skulls. The predicted coarse skulls are then upsampled to $512 \times 512 \times Z$ using spline interpolation. To learn a smooth voxel arrangement, another autoencoder (the same as the autoencoder used for skull shape completion in the first step) takes as input a random $128 \times 128 \times 64$ patch cropped from the upsampled coarse skull. The ground truth is the corresponding patch cropped from the complete skull in the training set. After training, the autoencoder runs on the upsampled coarse skulls in the test set to produce the final completed and voxel-rearranged high-resolution skulls.

For comparison with the above approaches, an autoencoder network is also trained using randomly cropped patches for patch-wise shape completion. From the training set, the autoencoder takes a randomly cropped patch from an original, high-resolution, defective skull as input and produces a complete skull patch as output. For a fair comparison, the training and inference strategy used in the patch-wise shape completion is the same as that of the voxel rearrangement-based method (as described in Sect. 3.1), in order to handle differently sized skull data. The autoencoder network used here is also the same as that used in the interpolation and voxel rearrangement-based method.

## 4.1 Interpolation, Patch-Wise Skull Shape Completion and Voxel Rearrangement

For the three approaches (interpolation, patch-wise skull shape completion and voxel rearrangement), the implants are obtained by subtracting the defective skulls in the test set from the final complete skulls generated by the algorithms. Experiments were carried out on the training and test set ($D_{100}$ and $D_{10}$) of *Task 3* of the AutoImplant 2021 Challenge.

**Table 1.** Mean values of the Dice Similarity Coefficient (DSC) and the Hausdorff Distance (HD, measured in mm) for the skulls and implants on the test set of *Task 3*.

| Methods | Skull ($D_{100}$) | | Skull ($D_{10}$) | | Implant ($D_{100}$) | | Implant ($D_{10}$) | |
|---|---|---|---|---|---|---|---|---|
| | $DSC$ | $HD$ | $DSC$ | $HD$ | $DSC$ | $HD$ | $DSC$ | $HD$ |
| Interpolation | 0.7547 | 24.4227 | 0.7546 | 23.5864 | 0.8151 | 32.5061 | 0.7135 | 42.3458 |
| Voxel rearrangement | 0.7529 | 37.1932 | 0.7574 | 24.9146 | 0.8135 | 30.8189 | 0.7563 | 28.0752 |
| Patch | 0.8587 | 16.8571 | 0.8493 | 27.0759 | 0.6178 | 27.0386 | – | – |

Table 1 shows the Dice similarity Coefficient (DSC) and the Hausdorff Distance (HD) of the completed skulls and implants for the three approaches: spline interpolation, voxel rearrangement and patch-wise skull shape completion on the test set ($D_{100}$ and $D_{10}$). Figure 5(a–d) shows the corresponding boxplots.

Figure 6 shows the skull shape completion results on $D_{100}$ (first row) and $D_{10}$ (second to fourth row) for the three approaches. We can see that even if quantitatively, the patch-wise skull shape completion method has the best scores regarding DSC and HD for the skull, the qualitative inspection of the completed skulls reveals that the patch-based completion method failed on $D_{10}$ and cannot completely restore the missing parts of the skulls on $D_{100}$. On the contrary, the autoencoder trained on downsampled skulls shows good generalization performance on both $D_{100}$ and $D_{10}$. For the skulls, despite that the DSC for the interpolation-based upsampling is quite close to that of the voxel rearrangement-based upsampling and that the HD of the interpolation-based upsampling is even smaller than that of the voxel rearrangement-based upsampling, Fig. 6 clearly shows the advantages of the voxel rearrangement-based upsampling in terms of the reconstruction quality (mainly the skull surface) between the two approaches. It should be noted that, due to the patch-wise training and inference scheme used for voxel rearrangement, we can see *stitching* lines on the contacting borders between neighboring patches (Fig. 6, last column), which is undesirable.

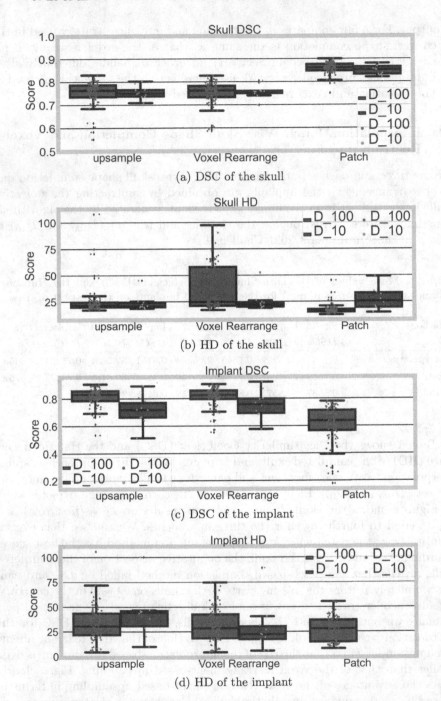

**Fig. 5.** Quantitative comparison (DSC, HD) of the three methods (upsample via spine interpolation, voxel rearrangement and patch-wise skull shape completion) on the test sets ($D_{100}$, $D_{10}$) of Task 3 of the AutoImplant challenge.

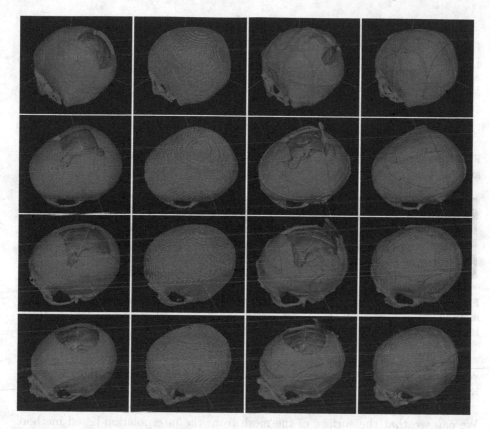

**Fig. 6.** From first to fourth column: the input defective skull, the completed skull from spline interpolation, patch-wise skull shape completion and voxel rearrangement (proposed).

Figure 7 shows a comparison of the triangulation results on the completed skull grids from the interpolation-based (a) and voxel rearrangement-based (b) approaches. It is evident that the mesh from the voxel-rearrangement based method is smooth, while the skull mesh from the interpolation-based method has a bumpy surface.

Figure 8 and Fig. 9 show the implants produced by the three approaches[5]. The patch-wise shape completion method failed on $D_{10}$ and therefore, the result is not shown in Fig. 9. We can see that post-processing using connected component analysis and morphological operations did not fully remove the artifacts on the implant. These artifacts (e.g., the non-implant piece on the implant borders in Fig. 8 and Fig. 9) can substantial increase the Hausdorff Distance (HD) between the prediction and ground truth, as reported in Table 1. The proposed

---

[5] The visualized implants in these figures, as well as the implants used for calculating the DSCs and HDs (Table 1, Fig. 5) are post-processed using the *denoise* script from the repository: https://github.com/Jianningli/voxel_rearrangement.

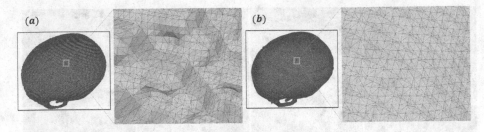

**Fig. 7.** Triangulation of the skull voxel grids produced by the interpolation-based (a) and voxel rearrangement-based (b) approaches.

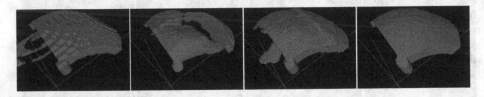

**Fig. 8.** From left to right: implant (voxel grid) obtained from the interpolation-based method, patch-wise skull shape completion and voxel rearrangement-based method. Rightmost: the ground truth implant (a test case selected from $D_{100}$).

voxel rearrangement-based method has the best performance on the implants regarding DSC.

Figure 10 illustrates the corresponding meshes of the implants shown in Fig. 9. We can see that the surface of the mesh from the interpolation-based method has obvious terracing artifacts. 3D printing of such a mesh will yield an implant with a rough surface, which is unusable in cranioplasty. On the contrary, the surface of the mesh from the proposed voxel rearrangement-based method is smooth and close to that of the ground truth.

## 4.2 Image Synthesis

As the image synthesis-based upsampling only works for images of certain sizes ($2^n$, e.g., $512 \times 512 \times 128$ or $512 \times 512 \times 256$), its quantitative performance (DSC and HD) is not evaluated on the whole test set and, therefore, not comparable to the other methods as reported in Table 1 and Fig. 5. However, qualitative results and comparison with a kd-tree-based image synthesis method for image upsampling will be given in this section.

Different from the proposed hash table-based image synthesis (Fig. 4(b)), the kd-tree-based method does not employ a binary encoding of the voxels. Instead, principal component analysis (PCA) is used to reduce the dimension of the feature vector (e.g., the $3^3 = 27$ neighboring voxels) to 20 in order to accelerate the search. The feature vectors from the template pyramid are used to construct a kd-tree and, correspondingly, the feature vectors from the coarse pyramid are also projected into the same principal component space. The NNS can, therefore,

**Fig. 9.** From left to right: implant (voxel grid) obtained from the interpolation-based method, voxel rearrangement-based method and ground truth (a test case selected from $D_{10}$).

**Fig. 10.** Triangulation results on the implant voxel grid. From left to right: interpolation-based method, voxel rearrangement-based method and ground truth.

be performed on a kd-tree structure, which is by magnitudes faster than a brute-force linear search strategy. It should be noted that the feature vectors will lose binariness after PCA is applied. Unlike the proposed hash table-based method, which performs essentially an approximated NNS, the kd-tree based method performs an exact NNS.

Figure 11 shows a comparison of the skulls from two image synthesis methods[6]. We can see the skull from the kd-tree-based method is of higher quality, which is understandable, as the kd-tree-based method does an exact NNS, whilst the hash table-based method does an approximated NNS. However, the memory consumption of the hash table-based method is much lower[7], as the binary feature vectors are stored as bit strings. Both approaches take less than three minutes to update all the required voxels for each level of the pyramid. Note that the synthesis process in this study is implemented to run on CPUs only. On GPUs, where the number of computing cores is usually large, the process could potentially be several magnitudes faster.

---

[6] The underlying network used to produce the coarse completed skull ($128 \times 128 \times 64$) is the same as that of the interpolation and voxel rearrangement-based method.

[7] E.g., 12% and 59% CPU memory consumption for the hash table and kd-tree-based method, respectively.

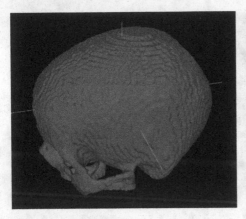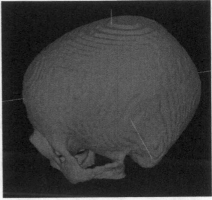

**Fig. 11.** High-resolution complete skull produced by the hash table-based (left) and kd-tree-based (right) image synthesis methods. Note: the skulls are synthesized from size $128 \times 128 \times 64$ to size $256 \times 256 \times 128$.

## 5  Discussion and Future Work

3D medical images are known to consume substantial computational resources (e.g., memory, number of FLOPs, etc.) in deep learning. By exploiting the characteristics, e.g., binariness and sparsity, of some specific images, computation requirement for processing these images can be effectively reduced. In our study, we have designed a tailored hash table-based method for nearest neighbor search, by making use of the binariness and spatial sparsity of the high-resolution skull images. However, the template skull image is selected randomly, which is suboptimal considering that the possibility of finding an exact match ($d_{HM} = 0$) in the template pyramid might be low for some cases, making the performance of the method unstable. In [3], the authors proposed to select the template image by matching each specific coarse image with a pool of candidate templates in a feature space of a trained autoencoder network. The template that has the smallest distance to the coarse image can be selected and used as the final template for synthesis. For our future work, using the same strategy[8] could potentially maximize the likelihood of finding the exact bit strings in the template pyramid for each bit string in the coarse template, which consequently increases the final reconstruction accuracy and would probably stabilize the performance of the method. It should be noted that the image synthesis-based method for image upsampling has not been fully evaluated in this study, partly because the method cannot synthesize arbitrarily-sized images. Another reason is that, while Algorithm 1, which lies at the core of the method, is stable, how to create the pyramid (Fig. 4(a)) and the hash table entries still remains open for discussion.

---

[8] The *feature space* script can be found in the following GitHub repository: https://github.com/Jianningli/voxel_rearrangement.

The voxel rearrangement-based method, on the contrary, has been sufficiently evaluated in our study. One unsolved issue for the method is the *stitching* lines between the contacting borders of patches. For future work, this problem could be solved by using the entire original skull images as the input of the network, instead of using a patch-wise training strategy. Tailored network architectures such as sparse convolutional neural networks could be designed to tackle the memory issue, taking into consideration the binariness and spatial sparsity of the skull data.

## 6 Conclusion

In our study, we have addressed the problem of high memory consumption of 3D medical images. Instead of processing the original high-resolution images directly, high-resolution outcome can be obtained indirectly in a coarse-to-fine fashion. Voxel rearrangement and image synthesis have proven to be effective in restoring the surface smoothness of the coarse output. Both approaches are general and can be used in other applications besides reconstruction, such as medical image segmentation.

**Acknowledgement.** This work was supported by the following funding agencies:
- CAMed (COMET K-Project 871132, see also https://www.medunigraz.at/camed/), which is funded by the Austrian Federal Ministry of Transport, Innovation and Technology (BMVIT) and the Austrian Federal Ministry for Digital and Economic Affairs (BMDW), and the Styrian Business Promotion Agency (SFG);
- The Austrian Science Fund (FWF) KLI 678-B31 (enFaced).

## References

1. Akil, M., Saouli, R., Kachouri, R., et al.: Fully automatic brain tumor segmentation with deep learning-based selective attention using overlapping patches and multi-class weighted cross-entropy. Med. Image Anal. **63**, 101692 (2020)
2. Chang, Y.Z., Wu, C.T., Yang, Y.H.: Three-dimensional deep learning to automatically generate cranial implant geometry (2021)
3. Dai, A., Ruizhongtai Qi, C., Nießner, M.: Shape completion using 3D-encoder-predictor CNNs and shape synthesis. In: Proceedings of the IEEE Conference on Computer Vision and Pattern Recognition, pp. 5868–5877 (2017)
4. Díaz García, J., Brunet Crosa, P., Navaro Álvaro, I., Vazquez Alcocer, P.P.: Down-sampling methods for medical datasets. In: Proceedings of the International Conferences Computer Graphics, Visualization, Computer Vision and Image Processing 2017 and Big Data Analytics, Data Mining and Computational Intelligence 2017, Lisbon, Portugal, 21–23 July 2017, pp. 12–20. IADIS Press (2017)
5. Graham, B., Engelcke, M., Van Der Maaten, L.: 3D semantic segmentation with submanifold sparse convolutional networks. In: Proceedings of the IEEE Conference on Computer Vision and Pattern Recognition, pp. 9224–9232 (2018)
6. Graham, B., van der Maaten, L.: Submanifold sparse convolutional networks. arXiv preprint arXiv:1706.01307 (2017)

7. Han, X., Li, Z., Huang, H., Kalogerakis, E., Yu, Y.: High-resolution shape completion using deep neural networks for global structure and local geometry inference. In: Proceedings of the IEEE International Conference on Computer Vision, pp. 85–93 (2017)
8. Kodym, O., Španěl, M., Herout, A.: Cranial defect reconstruction using cascaded CNN with alignment. In: Li, J., Egger, J. (eds.) AutoImplant 2020. LNCS, vol. 12439, pp. 56–64. Springer, Cham (2020). https://doi.org/10.1007/978-3-030-64327-0_7
9. Kodym, O., Španěl, M., Herout, A.: Skull shape reconstruction using cascaded convolutional networks. Comput. Biol. Med. **123**, 103886 (2020)
10. Li, J., et al.: Automatic skull defect restoration and cranial implant generation for cranioplasty. Med. Image Anal. **73**, 102171 (2021)
11. Li, J., Egger, J.: Dataset descriptor for the AutoImplant cranial implant design challenge. In: Li, J., Egger, J. (eds.) AutoImplant 2020. LNCS, vol. 12439, pp. 10–15. Springer, Cham (2020). https://doi.org/10.1007/978-3-030-64327-0_2
12. Li, J., Pepe, A., Gsaxner, C., von Campe, G., Egger, J.: A baseline approach for AutoImplant: the MICCAI 2020 cranial implant design challenge. arXiv preprint arXiv:2006.12449 (2020)
13. Li, J., et al.: AutoImplant 2020-first MICCAI challenge on automatic cranial implant design. IEEE Trans. Med. Imaging **40**(9), 2329–2342 (2021)
14. Riegler, G., Osman Ulusoy, A., Geiger, A.: OctNET: learning deep 3D representations at high resolutions. In: Proceedings of the IEEE Conference on Computer Vision and Pattern Recognition, pp. 3577–3586 (2017)
15. Wang, P.S., Liu, Y., Guo, Y.X., Sun, C.Y., Tong, X.: O-CNN: octree-based convolutional neural networks for 3D shape analysis. ACM Trans. Graph. (TOG) **36**(4), 1–11 (2017)

# A U-Net Based System for Cranial Implant Design with Pre-processing and Learned Implant Filtering

Hamza Mahdi[1] , Allison Clement[1] , Evan Kim[1], Zachary Fishman[1] ,
Cari M. Whyne[1,3], James G. Mainprize[1,2] , and Michael R. Hardisty[1,3]( )

[1] Sunnybrook Research Institute, Toronto, ON, Canada
michael.hardisty@sunnybrook.ca
[2] Calavera Surgical Design Inc., Toronto, ON, Canada
[3] Division of Orthopaedic Surgery, University of Toronto, Toronto, ON, Canada

**Abstract.** Craniomaxillofacial skeletal (CMFS) reconstructive surgeries require patient specific implants that reproduce pre-injury 3D geometries, often pre-injury geometry is not available and the implant design must be estimated from the remaining skull that contains defects.

A pipeline was created to automate patient specific implant design geometries suitable for post-injury segmentations. This investigation was done as part of the MICCAI AutoImplant Grand Challenge 2021. The challenge included two datasets; SkullBreak (clinically representative synthetic defects) and SkullFix (uniform synthetic defects).

The developed pipeline consisted of: cropping the skull geometry, prediction of intact skull geometry using a U-Net style encoder/decoder, binary subtraction of the predicted intact skull and defect skull to create a candidate implant, and post processing filtering. Changes in performance of the algorithm were investigated by varying 3 stages within the workflow: pre-processing, the dataset used to train the U-Net, and the post-processing filtering (spherical topological, or a U-Net trained filtering network).

The dataset used for training had the largest effect on the performance of the algorithm, with the SkullBreak trained networks generalizing better than the SkullFix trained algorithms. The spherical topological post process filtering was comparable to a network trained to filter the implant directly. The image cropping method also influenced the final predictive results. Our best performing model for the Task 3 test sets had a DSC = 0.88 ± 0.14.

The trained algorithms present a useful step towards an automated pipeline for generating implants, suitable for integration into a clinical pipeline that could increase reconstruction fidelity and dramatically decrease the cost of design.

Supported by the Canadian Institute for Health Research, INOVAIT, Biotalent, and Calavera Surgical.

H. Mahdi and A. Clement—Authors contributed equally to the paper.

J. Li and J. Egger (Eds.): AutoImplant 2021, LNCS 13123, pp. 63–79, 2021.
https://doi.org/10.1007/978-3-030-92652-6_6

**Keywords:** Craniofacial surgery · Deep learning · Patient-specific implants

# 1   Introduction

Defects to the craniomaxillofacial skeleton (CMFS) requiring reconstruction can occur from deformity, tumour resection or trauma. The CMFS plays a functional role (protecting the brain and providing bio-mechanical support for mastication and ocular tissues) as well as a cosmetic role that has a profound effect on psycho-social well-being. The clinical goal of CMFS reconstruction is to restore pre-injury bone geometry and appearance. Reconstruction of the CMFS can be hindered by a lack of a target patient specific geometry, particularly in the cases where pre-injury 3D computed tomography (CT) imaging studies of the intact skull would most likely not be available. Reliable 3D information to guide surgical planning and direct pre/intra-operative implant shaping.

Designing patient specific CMFS implants is the most straightforward in cases where intact pre-injury CT imaging is available. Intact skull imaging may exist in cases involving brain surgery and tumour resection; however in reconstruction for trauma, pre-injury imaging is unlikely to exist. Mirroring the uninjured side to provide guidance has been used as a strategy to reconstruct small unilateral defects with effective cosmesis and limited design effort. For bilateral defects and large defects, the design challenge becomes much greater. Currently, hours of design time may be required to manually reconstruct skull geometry with multiple iterations requiring clinical input. This motivates the development of automated methods that can generate intact skull geometry from skulls containing bony defects. An automated data-driven method applying the latest advances in machine learning provides the opportunity to rapidly create CMFS implants, while also potentially increasing the accuracy of the reconstruction in creating the designs. This investigation was written as part the 2nd MICCAI AutoImplant Grand Challenge in 2021, and is part of ongoing work at Sunnybrook Research Institute aimed at developing technology to improve CMFS reconstruction.

# 2   Datasets

The SkullBreak and SkullFix datasets [7] were both used in training, along with test sets provided as part of the 2nd MICCAI AutoImplant challenge in 2021. SkullBreak and SkullFix were created by segmenting bone from CT imaging of subjects without defects in the skull. The datasets did not contain the original medical imaging, only the label-fields. This segmentation created a 3D skull geometry where each pixel was labeled as either bone (1) or non-bone (0). Defects within the skull geometry were then created by artificially removing areas of the skull geometry. The removed region of the skull was then defined as the implant and the remaining skull as the defect skull. The primary differences between these two datasets were the orientation of the skull and the method of defect injection.

## 2.1   SkullFix

The SkullFix dataset was created as part of the 1st MICCAI AutoImplant grand challenge in 2020 from an open source collection of head-CT images (CQ500) [2]. The dataset consisted of 100 skull geometries, for which the slice spacing, head position and field of view varied. The field of view spanned the skull apex to the skull base, with some cases extending to portions of the neck. Volumes were non uniform in size ($512 \times 512 \times Z$, where $Z$ slices ranged from 150–300). Skulls were unaligned and the defects were nearly all localized to the posterior aspect of the skull. The defect shape was generally composed of circles and rectangle shapes, representing cranioplasty surgeries.

## 2.2   SkullBreak

The SkullBreak dataset [7] aimed to create synthetic skull defects that were more "clinically relevant" than the SkullFix dataset defects. The SkullBreak defects had more irregular shapes to be more representative of traumatic skull fractures. The skulls in the dataset were already uniformly aligned, resampled to isotropic voxel size, and cropped to the Frankfurt plane (the horizontal plane connecting the bottom of the eye and the ear canal) [7]. The dataset consisted of skull volumes (size $= 512 \times 512 \times 512$ voxels, 114 Training, 20 Test), with 5 defect types assigned to each unique complete skull (parieto-temporal unilateral, fronto-orbital unilateral, bilateral, and 2 random defects; total 570 Training, 100 Test). The defects were created by binary shape subtraction and defect border smoothing.

## 2.3   Challenge Test Datasets

The challenge datasets consisted of 3 distinct test sets that corresponded with 3 separated task submissions. Task 1 and Task 3 corresponded with the SkullBreak and SkullFix datasets. Task 2 was composed of skull geometry from CMFS reconstruction patients, where imaging and ground truth were created as part of the clinical care, providing excellent quality ground truth shape. An important note about the volumes is that for the purposes of anonymization, the facial bones were removed from the skull segmentations of this dataset (e.g. nasal, orbital, maxillary). Task 2 will test the generalizability of algorithms trained with synthetic defects in their application to clinical cases.

## 3   Methods

An automated workflow for the generation of implants for the cranium is presented in this investigation (Fig. 1). The approach involves the input of a damaged skull volume (with incorporated defects) as a binary label-field. The input defect binary label-field was cropped to include only the skull (two cropping methods were investigated), re-sampled to a consistent grid and then passed through a U-net to predict complete skulls. A U-Net (convolutional neural network, CNN) based algorithm was implemented to generate implant geometry. This structure was chosen based on the extensive scholarship applying convolutional deep networks to a variety of tasks related to implant generation (medical image segmentation, filtering, disease diagnosis, generation of synthetic medical image data) [3,11]. The complete skulls are then compared to the defect skulls to generate an implant based on subtraction. The implant is post-processed by smoothing and filtering (two filtering methods were investigated: (1) topological and (2) learned filtering). The algorithm was trained against both the SkullBreak and SkullFix datasets and tested against the three challenge tasks.

### 3.1 Preprocessing

**Cropping.** Head CT scans usually extend beyond the cranial vault. To speed up the training process and avoid training on regions with no relevant information, skull volumes were cropped based on image-specific calculated bounding boxes. The bounding boxes were generated using two methods: (1) zero cropping and (2) peak projection cropping. A visual example of the two cropping methods can be seen in Fig. 1.

In both cropping methods, the useful region was defined by a bounding box enclosing all non-zero voxels in the x and y directions. In the first cropping method (zero-cropping), the z-direction cropping enclosed all non-zero voxels similar to the x-y directions. For unaligned skulls, or different anatomic coverage (e.g., including or excluding maxilla), the second cropping method (peak-projection cropping) may reduce some irrelevant anatomy without a full registration module. In this method, the cropping was the same as the zero cropping, save for the inferior portion of the skull. Here, the skull base was located by a maximum-projection. A projection vector of the bone in the z-direction was found by performing matrix summation along the x and y directions. The skull base was assumed to be at the line where the most bone (peak projection) was located. Volumes were then truncated to the skull base.

In both cropping methods, a safety distance (8 voxels) was added to the apex and base of the skull to account for cases where the defect included the apex or the base of the skull.

**Resampling.** The cropped skulls were down-sampled and rescaled to a standard volume ($192 \times 256 \times 128$ volume, in Medial-Lateral $\times$ Anterior-Posterior $\times$ Superior-Inferior, respectively). The cropped skulls were rescaled to fit the pre-defined volume using a volume specific scaling factor along each axis.

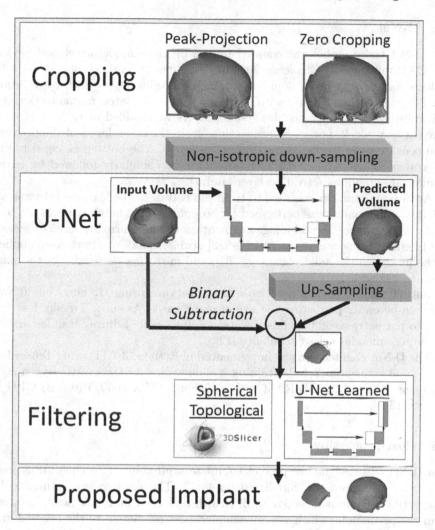

**Fig. 1.** Overview of the workflow for automated implant generation. 1) cropping (either by the peak-projection method or the zero-cropping method). 2) Non-isotropic down-sampling. 3) The input skull with defect is then placed into a U-Net to predict the full skull volume. 4) The prediction of the complete skull is up-sampled, and a binary subtraction of the skull with defect input and the predicted volume is used to create the implant segmentation. 5) Filtering is applied to the implant (either with spherical topological filters or via a U-Net learned method). 6) The proposed implant geometry is generated.

## 3.2  U-Net

The U-Net based model was adapted from a previous model developed for the MICCAI AutoImplant Challenge 2020 [9]. This model consisted of 5 layers with 8 filters for the first level, doubling for each following layer. Each convolution had 3D convolutional layers with kernels $(3 \times 3 \times 3)$. Batch normalization, an activation layer (ReLu) and MaxPooling layers were added at the end of each convolutional block. Long skip connections from the down levels of the network were concatenated to the corresponding up-layers. The bottleneck consisted of two convolutional layers with 32 filters. This was similarly followed by batch normalization and an activation layer (ReLu).

An Adam optimizer was used to train the network. The learning rate was set to 0.001 and training was performed for 30 epochs. The batch size was set to a single skull volume. To add image augmentation, randomized anterior-posterior and lateral shifting was performed ($[-2, 2]$ voxels), small rotations were applied to the images in the axial plane $[-5°, 5°]$, and mirroring (left-right) of the skull volumes was added.

Initially, dice loss was used as a loss function during training, but it was found to be under predicting the size of many cases. As such, Tversky loss was used to put extra weight on false positives (alpha $= 0.7$) during training and to better accommodate class imbalance [12].

The U-Net architecture was implemented in Python (3.7.11) using Tensorflow (2.4.1) and keras-gpu (2.4.3). Training was done on a 3.8 GHz AMD Ryzen 2600 processor (6 cores) 32 GB RAM with a GeForce GTX 1660Ti (6 GB) GPU in Ubuntu 18.04.

## 3.3  Post-processing

The U-Net was designed to predict complete skull volumes, necessitating post-processing to isolate the "predicted implant". The implant was estimated by subtracting the input defective skull (which had been morphologically dilated) from the prediction (which was up-sampled post-prediction to the original grid size) to mask out the remaining bone. To ensure a reasonably tight bounding box containing the implant, the voxels were thresholded to 0.7 to avoid including low- to mid-probability predictions outside the like implant volume. The implant was then binarized by thresholding predicted probabilities at 0.5 within that bounding box. To further clean out any noisy outputs, random small noisy objects were excluded using a 3D connected components[1] filter that extracts and labels binary connected objects.

**Spherical Topological Filter:** The implants in training sets for challenge 1 (SkullBreak) and 3 (SkullFix) were confined to the cranium, meaning we could assume the implants have spherical topology and smooth bony prominences. Similar to our groups approach to the AutoImplant 2020 Challenge, a spherical

---

[1] pypi.org/project/connected-components-3d/.

topological filter was applied. The filter closes interior holes and removes all but the largest connected component. Then the implant was smoothed (Gaussian, $\sigma^2 = 0.5 \times 0.5 \times 0.5\,\text{mm}$, with all other parameters set to default values, consistent for all implants) followed by binary closing and a level set based anti-aliasing filter [13]. This filter was applied from a shape analysis extension ([1]) within 3D Slicer.[2] Parameters for the filter were based on experience with a previous pipeline for CMFS implant design developed by our group.

**Learned (network) Filter:** A new addition to our approach this year is filtering with a learning-paradigm based filter, instead of using classical filters such as the spherical topological filter. The goal of using this filter is to overcome the limitations of classical filtering which need customized parameters for optimal processing. A deep learning approach to filtering may help generalize over a multitude of cases without having to customize parameters which makes optimal uniform post-processing possible. Such approach would only be limited by the amount of data present and can be continuously improved, unlike classical algorithms which do not change when presented with different types of data. In this paper, we used a U-net approach (similar to the base implant prediction task) to learn the filter. More details on the network and training data are discussed in Sect. 4.3.

### 3.4 Analysis

The generated implants were compared to ground truth implants in validation sets within both the SkullBreak and SkullFix datasets. The validation set for SkullBreak consisted of implants #100 to #113. For SkullFix, the validation set consisted of implants #88 to #100. The Dice Similarity Coefficient (DSC) and Hausdorff Distance (HD) at the original resolution were used to characterize agreement. Additionally, for the AutoImplant Challenge tasks, border DSC and the 95 percentile HD were reported as they were calculated during challenge evaluation. In addition to quantitative methods, defect skulls with generated implants in place were visualized (Fig. 2).[3]

## 4    Experiments and Results

Changes in performance of the algorithm were investigated by varying the three stages within the workflow: varying the dataset used to train the U-Net, choice of prepossessing (peak-projection cropping, or zero cropping), and varying the post-processing filtering (spherical topological, or a U-Net learned).

---

[2] www.slicer.org.

[3] https://github.com/OldaKodym/evaluation_metrics/blob/master/metrics.py.

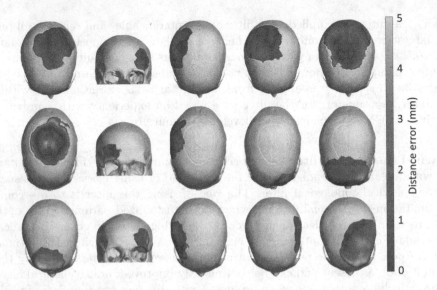

**Fig. 2.** SkullBreak dataset validation results of the peak-projection cropping network after filtering with the topological filter (HD = 10.08, DSC = 0.78). The distance from the estimated implant to the true implant is mapped on a scale from 0 to 5 mm. From left to right, the skull defects are arranged by region: Bilateral, Fronto-orbital, Parieto-temporal, Random 1, and Random 2.

## 4.1 Comparison of Different Training Datasets

We investigated the effect that the different training data (SkullBreak and Skull-Fix) had on the performance of the algorithm. We hypothesized that networks trained with the SkullBreak dataset would have superior performance and generalizability based on examination of the datasets and on their descriptions. The U-Nets were trained with consistent pre- and post-processing to isolate the effect of the training data on the skull filling U-Net. Specifically zero-cropping was done for preprocessing and spherical topological filtering for postprocessing. Performance and generalizability were assessed by comparison with validation sets from both SkullBreak and SkullFix regardless of the training data used.

The SkullBreak trained skull-filling U-Net generalized better than the Skull-Fix trained network (Table 1). The SkullFix trained network outperformed the SkullBreak trained network when tested against SkullFix, however the Skull-Fix trained network failed to generalize to the SkullBreak test with a dramatic reduction in performance with many failed implant predictions.

## 4.2 Comparison of Cropping Methods

As noted above, when a network trained on SkullBreak is applied to the unregistered skulls in SkullFix, the predictions are degraded. Similarly, when trained on SkullFix, the performance on the registered SkullBreak data is poor. Towards

**Table 1.** DSC of the predicted implants compared to the ground truth implants by the zero-cropping model. Comparison of networks trained with SkullBreak and SkullFix data on the validation sets from both SkullBreak and SkullFix groups.

| | Validation | | | |
|---|---|---|---|---|
| | SkullBreak | | SkullFix | |
| | Mean | Std | Mean | Std |
| SkullBreak trained | 0.79 | 0.09 | 0.90 | 0.05 |
| SkullFix trained | 0.11 | 0.19 | 0.92 | 0.02 |

**Table 2.** Effect of different cropping modes on implant performance (topological filtering) in the validation splits of the SkullBreak and SkullFix datasets

| | HD | | DSC | |
|---|---|---|---|---|
| | Mean | Std | Mean | Std |
| SkullBreak peak-project | 10.08 | 6.29 | 0.78 | 0.14 |
| SkullFix peak-project | 11.56 | 7.86 | 0.84 | 0.06 |
| SkullBreak zero | 9.13 | 5.73 | 0.79 | 0.07 |
| SkullFix zero | 4.15 | 1.02 | 0.88 | 0.03 |

addressing this issue, two different cropping methods (zero-cropping and peak-cropping) were investigated as changes to the preprocessing before input to the U-Net. In principle, the peak-cropping should reduce some of the variability in the SkullFix dataset. The zero-cropping method was shown to have a slight edge in performance on the validation tests (Table 2) and in the challenge tasks as discussed below in Sect. 4.4.

**Table 3.** Effect of different filtering modes on implant performance (inference done from the peak-projection model) in the validation splits of the SkullBreak and SkullFix datasets

| | HD | | DSC | |
|---|---|---|---|---|
| | Mean | Std | Mean | Std |
| SkullBreak unfiltered | 22.57 | 9.83 | 0.78 | 0.14 |
| SkullBreak topological | 10.08 | 6.29 | 0.78 | 0.14 |
| SkullBreak learned | 9.96 | 5.91 | 0.74 | 0.14 |
| SkullFix unfiltered | 59.31 | 21.88 | 0.82 | 0.08 |
| SkullFix topological | 11.56 | 7.86 | 0.84 | 0.06 |
| SkullFix learned | 10.51 | 5.88 | 0.81 | 0.07 |

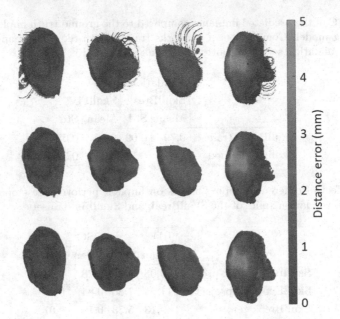

**Fig. 3.** Performance of filtering modes on a subset of the SkullBreak validation dataset. The distance from the estimated implant to the true implant is mapped on a scale from 0 to 5 mm. The filtering options top to bottom: unfiltered, topological filtering, learned (network) filtering. The implants left to right are #101, #102, #103, #104.

## 4.3  Comparison of Implant Filtering Methods

Following basic post-processing, filtering was needed due to rough edges seen on the implants as shown in Fig. 3. Rough edges and spurious implant predictions were noted by investigators in last year's AutoImplant challenge, resulting from post-process filtering (morphological opening prior to isolation of the largest connected component [4]). To address the post-processing challenges, this investigation considered 2 different options, a learned filter and a spherical topological filter. A learned filter was created that used the same U-Net architecture as described above. The input unfiltered implants used were those predicted by the U-Net (trained with peak-projection cropped SkullBreak dataset, 100:14 testing and validation split). The ground truth implants were used as the desired output. The rationale for implementing this approach was the possibility of improving post-processing using a data driven approach. This can specialize filtering to a specific task and improve with larger data sets, in contrast to the pre-engineered topological filtering described above, while allowing the Skull generating U-Net to be trained with separate datasets. Both filters show dramatic improvement over the unfiltered predictions (Fig. 3, Table 3), with respect to HD, with minor losses in DSC performance. Filtered implants achieved HD that were at least twice as good as the unfiltered ones. The filtering performance for both methods was comparable for the validation datasets. The topological filter slightly outperformed the learned filter on competition Tasks 1 and 3 (Table 3).

## 4.4    Performance on AutoImplant Challenge

Based on the above comparison studies and the preliminary results we submitted candidate algorithm results to Tasks, 1, 2, and 3 using peak-projection cropping (Table 4) and zero-cropping (Table 5) both with topological filtering.

**Table 4.** Performance of the peak-projection cropping model on the AutoImplant 2021 challenge. All implants were passed through the topological filter before evaluation.

|  | DSC | | bDSC | | HD95 | |
|---|---|---|---|---|---|---|
|  | Mean | Std | Mean | Std | Mean | Std |
| Task 1 | 0.78 | 0.09 | 0.81 | 0.07 | 3.42 | 1.37 |
| Task 2 | 0.38 | 0.15 | 0.33 | 0.15 | 51.24 | 81.76 |
| Task 3 | 0.85 | 0.07 | 0.85 | 0.06 | 2.78 | 1.06 |

**Table 5.** Performance of the zero-cropping model on the AutoImplant 2021 challenge. All implants were passed through the topological filter before evaluation.

|  | DSC | | bDSC | | HD95 | |
|---|---|---|---|---|---|---|
|  | Mean | Std | Mean | Std | Mean | Std |
| Task 1 | 0.76 | 0.10 | 0.82 | 0.07 | 3.80 | 2.20 |
| Task 2 | 0.30 | 0.17 | 0.31 | 0.19 | 71.42 | 87.02 |
| Task 3 | 0.88 | 0.14 | 0.93 | 0.12 | 3.59 | 12.55 |

Predictions from the SkullBreak and SkullFix trained networks were submitted to Task 1 and Task 3 respectively because of the training data corresponding to the task. Predictions from the SkullBreak trained networked were submitted to Task 2 because of the demonstrated superior generalizability in the above comparison studies. Quantitative results were reported directly from the challenge outcomes and qualitative assessments were done by visualization.

Performance was found to be acceptable for Tasks 1 and 3 of the AutoImplant challenge (Table 4). However, Task 2, the clinical data set, was not well predicted by this algorithm with any of the variations submitted. All implants generated in Task 2 had poor DSC scores. Although some cases yielded reasonable results when qualitatively judged by their appearance, other cases when visualized were shown to have completely failed with respect to shape and location (Fig. 4). Of the 2 candidate cropping techniques submitted the peak-projection method was marginally superior quantitatively however the zero-cropping method created implants that looked qualitatively better when visualized (Figs. 4 and 5).

The zero-cropping method was shown to be equivalent or superior to the peak-projection method save for the HD scores in Task 3, wherein the peak-cropping likely reduced the variability of the anatomy in the Task 3 (equivalent to SkullFix) dataset.

Examples of Task 2 using the peak-cropping approach are shown in Fig. 4. Although the implants' performance seems acceptable in several cases, the average DSC score is 0.38. This is attributed in part to a case of complete failure (top row, 3rd implant left to right), and a case of partial failure (second row, 2nd implant left to right).

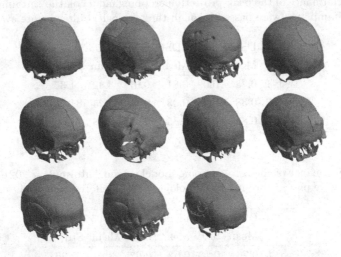

**Fig. 4.** Performance of the peak-projection cropping model on Task 2 of the AutoImplant challenge. Green regions represent the filtered predicted implant (Color figure online)

For Task 2 using the zero-cropping approach, examples are shown in Fig. 5. This approach appeared to perform worse than the peak-cropping method (0.30 vs. 0.38), Suggesting that better registration and volume matching is required for Task 2. Alternatively, augmenting the dataset with increased position variability may help. As well, the cropped facial feature due to de-identification as this dataset likely affected performance of the prediction.

## 5   Discussion and Future Work

The zero-cropping U-Net trained with the SkullBreak dataset with classical filtering was found to be the all-around best performing algorithm. However, no single algorithm combination yielded superior performance when considered against all test sets. As expected, the dataset used to train the model had a large influence on algorithm performance. For instance, the best performance for Task

1 and Task 3 were the SkullBreak and SkullFix trained (matching the test and validation sets), this was also consistent with the comparison study. However, the SkullBreak trained models had superior generalizability to those trained on the SkullFix dataset (outperforming the SkullFix trained model on the test sets and having better relative performance on the opposite dataset's test set). This highlights the importance of the increased variability of implant shape and location as found within the SkullBreak dataset in training algorithms for CMFS implant shape generation. This finding highlights the difficulty of the overarching goal of this AutoImplant MICCAI challenge to create useful synthetic implant shapes combined with limited clinical data to develop algorithms suitable for generating implant shapes in skulls with defects. This also draws attention to the potential of data augmentation, as while the two datasets had a similar number of skull geometries, the SkullBreak dataset contained more augmentation with respect to defect shape and location.

Consistent with this finding was our group's paper in last year's AutoImplant Challenge [9]; last year's model performed slightly better than this year (0.904 DSC vs. 0.88 DSC) on Task 3. This can be attributed to using additional defect (spherical and cubic) augmentations in last year's model [9] which significantly increased the size of our training set as opposed to this year. Further Consistent with this result, it was shown that skull shape augmentation also boosts performance for this task [8]. This suggests that augmentation of the geometry and implant shape could further improve performance in Task 1 and Task 3, however these enhancements were not the focus of this investigation.

It was also noted that the poor predictions tended to occur in larger sized defects (Fig. 6). One potential solution may be to augment the dataset with

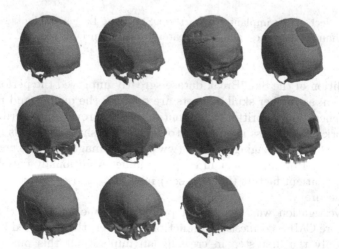

**Fig. 5.** Skulls with predicted implants submitted to Task 2 of the MICCAI 2021 challenge. Predictions for Test set based on clinical data created using the SkullBreak trained with Zero Cropping method.

larger defects to aid prediction. The predictions for large implants tended to have lower probabilities (especially towards the centre of the implant), suggesting that a threshold lower than 0.5 may have been appropriate. Instead, a dynamic thresholding based on contextual information such as defect size could help with this issue.

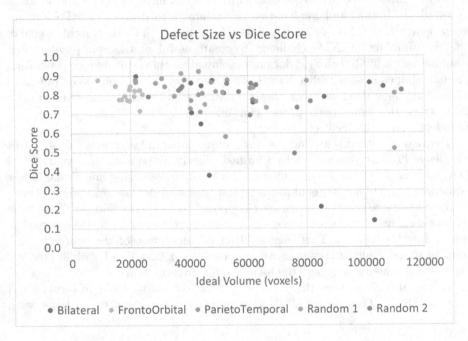

**Fig. 6.** The effect of the implant size on the DSC score. Larger implants seem to fail more often than smaller ones, and had greater variation in DSC scores.

The addition of the SkullBreak dataset greatly improved the performance of this algorithm; as further skull datasets are created, the quality and robustness of CMFS generation algorithms will continue to improve. As described in our previous work [9], progress is on-going to curate and share hundreds more head CTs from the Cancer Imaging Archive (www.cancerimagingarchive.net) towards improving the performance of skull shape training. Additionally patient-specific metadata for patient factors (i.e. age, sex) may also be used to further improve prediction accuracy.

This investigation was focused on predicting bone geometry that can be used to restore CMFS cosmesis and function, however, the predicted bone shape represents only the first step in creating an implant for this purpose. Additional considerations are required to inform modification of a clinically relevant implant shape beyond matching the bone shape. For instance, the appropriate thickness of an implant may depend on implant strength and weight. Further, the shape modifications may be required to enable an implant to be "insertable" into a defect. Complex matching of irregular margins where the designed implant extends under the interior margin are not clinically feasible solutions because the implant would be impossible to place (Fig. 7). Further modifications include the insertion of drainage holes or tabs to secure the implant to the skull surface [10]. Such post processing considerations motivated our use of filters after initial prediction of the implants with the U-Net. Specifically, we investigated the concept of training a filter to post process implant predictions based on a complete skull prediction. The use of this post-processing network could potentially be extended to such modifications through training on clinical implants (such features cannot be directly learned from examples of intact geometry). In this, we propose a 2-step process of (1) learning to predict the bone shape, followed by (2) learning to refine the design to yield a clinically relevant implant. This architecture can take advantage of the relatively large amounts of intact skull data to train the model for the bone shape, with subsequent training on what could be a simpler task of implant modification with smaller datasets of implant design examples.

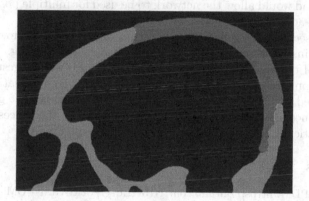

**Fig. 7.** Sagittal cross-section of an accurate implant prediction that is not clinically usable as the posterior-inferior margin prevents insertion into the defect.

The learned network filter's performance was comparable to that of the "classical" topological filter. Both filters were able to greatly improve the HD score for implants compared to unfiltered implants. The topological filter had a slight advantage quantitatively. However, with more data, the learned filter has the potential to not only "clean up" the predicted implant, but also possibly correct the geometry of the prediction if context information (i.e. surgical indication, broken skull geometry) is given to the filter.

The investigation was limited by several key factors, most notably that the Task 2 results for the algorithm were poor. This was likely due to differences between the training sets and the clinical data test set. The real patient cases presented were anonymized by removing the facial bones (whereas the training sets used in the development of the algorithm contained intact facial bones).

In several cases, the estimated implant designs had significant errors for CMFS defects that were near the missing facial bones. In clinical practice, the patient's implant design would be conducted with permission from the surgeon or healthcare institution, and would not require anonymization. In other open data sets, such as the SICAS Medical Image Repository (www.smir.ch), head CTs are de-identified by only removing the facial soft-tissue and leaving the skull shape intact. Other features that may have differed between the real and synthetic domains could be the result of variation in CT scanner hardware used, institutional acquisition protocols, skull orientation or defect shape. To improve the U-Net based algorithm performance, a suitable approach would be to retrain the decoding feature layers in the U-Net with a limited set of clinical data, consistent with domain adaptation approaches demonstrated in the literature [5,6]. Future work can also explore identifying a primary defect. In real clinical cases, there can be secondary defects that require reconstruction. Secondary implant estimation could be done by the U-net itself by post-processing with the learned filter. In addition to importing a predicted implant, the broken skull can also be concatenated as an input. This secondary learned filter could provide contextual information, and would allow the network to be used for multiple post-processing procedures, in addition to filtering.

The proposed implant generating algorithm was shown to perform well when compared against test sets similar to those used in its training. The modest performance of the algorithm applied to the clinical dataset suggests a need for further development and re-training with clinical data. By integrating the algorithm developed within this investigation into a framework for the generation of implants, engineers and surgeons can ultimately improve the process of implant design, dramatically decreasing time and improving quality.

# References

1. SPHARM-PDM. https://github.com/NIRALUser/SPHARM-PDM
2. Chilamkurthy, S., et al.: Development and validation of deep learning algorithms for detection of critical findings in head CT scans (2018)
3. Çiçek, Ö., Abdulkadir, A., Lienkamp, S.S., Brox, T., Ronneberger, O.: 3D U-net: learning dense volumetric segmentation from sparse annotation. In: Ourselin, S., Joskowicz, L., Sabuncu, M.R., Unal, G., Wells, W. (eds.) MICCAI 2016. LNCS, vol. 9901, pp. 424–432. Springer, Cham (2016). https://doi.org/10.1007/978-3-319-46723-8_49
4. Ellis, D.G., Aizenberg, M.R.: Deep learning using augmentation via registration: 1st place solution to the AutoImplant 2020 challenge. In: Li, J., Egger, J. (eds.) AutoImplant 2020. LNCS, vol. 12439, pp. 47–55. Springer, Cham (2020). https://doi.org/10.1007/978-3-030-64327-0_6
5. Gholami, A., et al.: A novel domain adaptation framework for medical image segmentation. In: Crimi, A., Bakas, S., Kuijf, H., Keyvan, F., Reyes, M., van Walsum, T. (eds.) BrainLes 2018. LNCS, vol. 11384, pp. 289–298. Springer, Cham (2019). https://doi.org/10.1007/978-3-030-11726-9_26
6. Javanmardi, M., Tasdizen, T.: Domain adaptation for biomedical image segmentation using adversarial training. In: 2018 IEEE 15th International Symposium on Biomedical Imaging (ISBI 2018), pp. 554–558. IEEE (2018)

7. Kodym, O., et al.: SkullBreak/SkullFix-dataset for automatic cranial implant design and a benchmark for volumetric shape learning tasks. Data Brief. **35**, 106902 (2021)
8. Li, J., et al.: AutoImplant 2020-first MICCAI challenge on automatic cranial implant design. IEEE Trans. Med. Imaging **40**(9), 2329–2342 (2021)
9. Mainprize, J.G., Fishman, Z., Hardisty, M.R.: Shape completion by U-Net: an approach to the AutoImplant MICCAI cranial implant design challenge. In: Li, J., Egger, J. (eds.) AutoImplant 2020. LNCS, vol. 12439, pp. 65–76. Springer, Cham (2020). https://doi.org/10.1007/978-3-030-64327-0_8
10. Pasick, C.M., Margetis, K., Santiago, G.F., Gordon, C., Taub, P.J.: Adult cranioplasty. J. Craniofac. Surg. **30**(7), 2138–2143 (2019)
11. Ronneberger, O., Fischer, P., Brox, T.: U-Net: convolutional networks for biomedical image segmentation. In: Navab, N., Hornegger, J., Wells, W.M., Frangi, A.F. (eds.) MICCAI 2015. LNCS, vol. 9351, pp. 234–241. Springer, Cham (2015). https://doi.org/10.1007/978-3-319-24574-4_28
12. Salehi, S.S.M., Erdogmus, D., Gholipour, A.: Tversky loss function for image segmentation using 3D fully convolutional deep networks. In: Wang, Q., Shi, Y., Suk, H.-I., Suzuki, K. (eds.) MLMI 2017. LNCS, vol. 10541, pp. 379–387. Springer, Cham (2017). https://doi.org/10.1007/978-3-319-67389-9_44
13. Styner, M., et al.: Framework for the statistical shape analysis of brain structures using SPHARM-PDM. Insight J. **1071**, 242 (2006)

# Sparse Convolutional Neural Network
# for Skull Reconstruction

Artem Kroviakov[1,2], Jianning Li[1,2,3(✉)], and Jan Egger[1,2,3]

[1] Institute of Computer Graphics and Vision, Graz University of Technology,
Inffeldgasse 16, 8010 Graz, Austria
{jianning.li,egger}@icg.tugraz.at
[2] Computer Algorithms for Medicine Laboratory (Café-Lab), 8010 Graz, Austria
[3] Institute for AI in Medicine (IKIM), University Hospital Essen, Girardetstraße 2,
45131 Essen, Germany

**Abstract.** Patient-specific implant (PSI) design is a challenging task
and requires a specialist, who will spend a significant amount of time
using computer aided design tools for implant creation, since patient-
specific skull features have to be accounted for. Automating this process
could potentially allow intraoperative PSI availability at a relatively low
cost. This work proposes to use a 3D Sparse Convolutional Neural Network (SCNN) to reconstruct complete skulls given defective skulls (i.e.,
skull shape completion) and extract implants by taking the difference
between them. With the help of recently published methods for sparse
convolutions, it is now possible to avoid the downsampling of the whole
skull volume, which is required for conventional dense 3D CNN applications proposed previously. Thus, the SCNN-based approach allows to
preserve the original skull geometry. The proposed pipeline includes a
supervised SCNN autoencoder network with data preprocessing steps,
which further exploit the sparse nature of a skull scan. The best setup
in our experiments achieves a Dice Score (DS) of 85.4%, a Border Dice
Score of 94.6%, Hausdorff Distance (HD) of 4.91 and 95th percentile
HD of 2.64 on the dataset for Task 3 of the AutoImplant 2021 challenge
(https://autoimplant2021.grand-challenge.org/). The results are comparable with a dense CNN counterpart which has significantly more parameters and requires downsampling and cropping of the skull image on 6GB
GPUs. The code is publicly available at https://github.com/akroviakov/
SparseSkullCompletion.

**Keywords:** Sparse Convolutional Neural Network (SCNN) · Shape
completion

## 1 Introduction

Patient specific implants (PSI) are custom-made implants, inferred from the
individual skull structure of a patient. PSI design invloves a specialist, high resolution computer tomographic scans, computer-aided design (CAD) tools, and

© Springer Nature Switzerland AG 2021
J. Li and J. Egger (Eds.): AutoImplant 2021, LNCS 13123, pp. 80–94, 2021.
https://doi.org/10.1007/978-3-030-92652-6_7

a substantial amount of time. Because of that, this process requires out-of-clinic production, making intraoperative solutions of low availability. Besides, during the implant design period, the skull of a patient may start its regenerative process, making it even more difficult to achieve best fit with the implant designed relying on the original defective skull.

With recent machine learning advances, it is now possible to automate the process with the help of Deep Convolutional Neural Networks (CNN) [1]. The main challenge for a conventional 3D CNN applications is the memory limitation, which usually requires the downsampling of the whole skull volume. This approach results in a loss of the information of the skull geometry during both downsampling and subsequent upsampling procedures. Existent solutions to the problem include a patch-wise training and inference scheme [2] and a coarse-to-fine framework [3,4]. These approaches, nevertheless, did not fully leverage the spatial sparsity of the skull volume within a CNN framework[1]. Conventional 3D dense CNN appears to be inefficient in both memory and speed aspects, as the voxel occupancy rate (VOR) of a skull scan tends to be less than 10% on average.

This work proposes a sparse convolution[2] based CNN (SCNN) for skull reconstruction. Unfortunately, popular deep learning frameworks such as TensorFlow, PyTorch and Keras do not support sparse convolutions and thus a suitable framework for SCNN had to be discovered. One of the main framework requirements for the task was the generative ability of the network. During initial exploration of sparse convolution frameworks, Minkowski Engine (ME) [6] (wrapped with PyTorch) was selected to be the basis of the proposed network, as it supports generative transpose convolution and convenient network construction.

The proposed SCNN is evaluated on a skull dataset of the AutoImplant challenge [7], which includes 100 skull volumes for training and 110 for testing. Out of these training cases, 96 skulls are used for network training and four skulls are used for validation.

## 2   Minkowski Engine

Minkowski Engine (ME) is an auto-differentiation library for sparse tensors [6], which works in combination with PyTorch layers and thus allows easy construction of neural networks (in this study, an autoencoder is constructed). ME takes advantage of the spatial sparsity of images, thus accelerating inference and minimizing memory consumption. Conventional dense CNNs, in comparison, lack efficiency when applied to spatially sparse data. Instead of conventional dense tensors, sparse tensors are used as input and output of the network and the network is therefore called "sparse tensor network". Such networks take sparse tensors as input, process them and generate sparse tensors as output. A sparse

---

[1] The work from J. Li. et al. [4] proposed a fast and memory-efficient nearest neighbor search solution for skull reconstruction, taking the advantage of the binariness and spatial sparsity of the skull images.

[2] Not to be confused with the sparse convolutional neural networks proposed in [5], which focused on model sparsity instead of data sparsity as in our work.

tensor itself is an extension of sparse matrix with non-zero entries being represented as a set of coordinates and associated features. A sparse tensor also has a coordinate manager, which is used for different operations on a tensor, such as subtraction, addition, etc. To perform these operations, sparse tensors must share the same coordinate manager. ME further supports all standard neural network layers such as multi-layer perceptrons (MLPs), non-linearities, convolution, normalizations and pooling operations. When dealing with sparse tensors in ME, there is no common notion of image *resolution* as in standard dense CNN, unless you want to convert it back to a dense tensor. The *size* of a sparse tensor depends on the number of points, which can be sampled arbitrarily from an image. Thus, unlike conventional CNNs, sparse CNNs' memory usage does not depend on the resolution of the volume and the memory usage of SCNN is close to linear to the number of input points sampled. This is hugely advantageous especially when processing large 3D images, whose memory consumption increases in a cubic manner in relation to their *resolution*.

## 2.1  Sparse Convolutions

A typical convolution layer extracts features by applying a certain filter and mapping the resulting feature into feature space. This filter, or kernel, slides through the whole image or volume and computes dot product between the kernel itself and the area or volume it covers. Such convolution layers are the essential part of CNN, as the overwhelming amount of computation inside the network is produced by these layers. However, for sparse problems, or for objects that live on a lower dimensionality level (i.e., submanifolds) than the space they are embedded in (e.g., lines in an image, line/surface in a volume), a conventional CNN would result in wasting of computation time and memory, while processing the empty regions of the input. To address this issue, Minkowski Engine (ME) adopts sparse convolution introduced in [8], and proposes generalized sparse convolution.

To generate output coordinates given the input coordinates, an input is convolved with a kernel and a mapping is generated to identify the relation between input and output. This mapping is called kernel map and it is defined as tuples of input and output indices. Given the input and output coordinates, their mapping and kernel weights, the generalized sparse convolution is calculated by iterating through the list of indice pairs:

$$x_u^{out} = \sum_{i \in \mathcal{N}^D(u, \mathcal{C}^{in})} W_i x_{u+i}^{in} \text{ for } u \in \mathcal{C}^{out} \tag{1}$$

where $\mathcal{C}^{in}$ is a set of input coordinates, $\mathcal{C}^{out}$ is a set of output coordinates, $x_u^{out}$ is $N^{out}$ dimensional feature vector in a D-dimensional space at $u$ coordinate, kernel weights are represented as $W \in \mathbb{R}^{K^D \times N^{out} \times N^{in}}$ (the weights are broken down into spatial weights with $K^D$ matrices of size $N^{out} \times N^{in}$ as $W_i$ for $|\{i\}_i| = K^D$) and $\mathcal{N}^D$ is a set of offsets that describe kernel shape. $\mathcal{N}^D(u, \mathcal{C}^{in}) = \{i | u + i \in \mathcal{C}^{in}, i \in \mathcal{N}^D\}$ denotes the set of offsets from the current center $u$ from $\mathcal{C}^{in}$.

For transposed generative sparse convolution [9] which are vital in the proposed network, the role of input and output coordinates is reversed. Further details on the implementation can be found in ME's original paper [6]. Generative process is achieved by upsampling of the volume, where certain coordinates will be pruned subsequently. At initial iterations, it is crucial to utilize target lookups to learn which voxels should not be pruned.

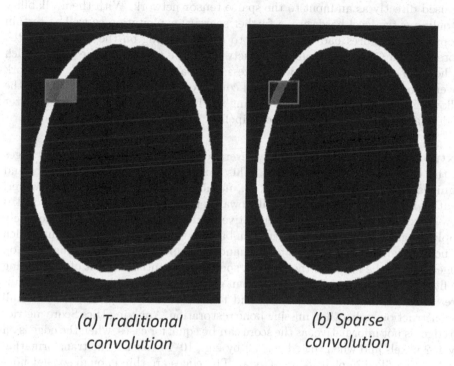

(a) Traditional convolution

(b) Sparse convolution

**Fig. 1.** Illustration of traditional (a) and sparse (b) convolution applied to the skull viewed on an axial slice. Note that the red area is involved in computation. (Color figure online)

Figure 1 shows a comparison between the traditional convolutions and sparse convolutions that are applied on a skull image. The red area on each image illustrates the region of interest (ROI) for the convolutional operations. We can see that for traditional CNNs (Fig. 1(a)), both the skull bone area and the background are involved in computation, while for sparse CNNs (Fig. 1(b)), the convolutions only operate on the area of skull bones. Considering the rather high rate of unoccupied voxels in an image volume of the skull, sparse convolutions are potentially effective in reducing the memory consumption in the skull reconstruction task compared to traditional convolutions, thus enabling a neural network to consume the entire skull geometry without downsampling.

# 3    Methods

## 3.1    Data Preprocessing and Postprocessing

Provided data contains skulls extracted from CT scans, that are stored in NRRD format. The voxel occupancy rate (VOR) of the provided scans is at most 9.81% with average being close to 6%. This is already highly sparse data and scans can be used directly as an input to the sparse tensor network. With the availability of only a entry level hardware, a further sparsity exploitation as well as certain cropping procedures had to be made to allow learning on the available GPU. Note that 16 GB of RAM allow the network to be trained on the CPU, which is, however, a significantly slower process, compared to on the GPU. This work covers mostly GPU based network and corresponding decisions of SCNN. In the following subsections, data preprocessing methods will be presented for a better understanding of the reconstruction pipeline.

**Extracting Edges.** We can further leverage sparsity, by considering only edges of the defective skull and implant. This way we preserve their geometry and significantly reduce the input size (i.e., number of points, see Fig. 2). However, shifting from using the original skulls towards using only the skull edges provokes new issues, such as the lack of generative performance, inability to adequately apply given metrics, and transformation back to the original filled implant, which is non-trivial. The generative performance is impaired when training only on edges, due to the fact that the network spends substantial amount of time trying to fit the reconstructed skull, rather than generate implant edges, as the implant area is only a fraction of the skull and thus the loss mostly comes from skull reconstruction rather than missing bone restoration. Applying Dice Score metrics to edges is not informative, as the score can be equal for cases, when the edge is off by 1–2 voxels and when the edge is off by e.g., 10–15 voxels. The transformation back to the filled implant is non-trivial. The edges are thin enough so that non-continuous edges are common. Taken into consideration of all these factors, it was decided to combine defective skull edges and the original filled implant to be the ground truth and use the defective skull edges as input, which basically solved all of the issues above. The skull edges hereby did not significantly contribute to the total number of points and affect the point generation, as the loss is now strongly affected by the filled implant. For edge extraction we perform morphological erosion with one iteration and XOR the result with the initial skull:

$$S_e = S_f \oplus (S_f \ominus) \tag{2}$$

$S_e$ stands for the extracted edges of the skull and $S_f$ stands for the original filled skull. $\oplus$ is the XOR operation and $\ominus$ is the morphological erosion. In Table 1 you can see the comparison of dataset's mean VOR before and after the edge extraction. Figure 2 shows a comparison of a skull slice before and after edge extraction. On top of each image shows the number of points of the corresponding skull.

**Table 1.** Comparison of VOR for different scan representations

| Scan data representation | Mean VOR |
|---|---|
| Default defective | 0.054 |
| Default complete | 0.059 |
| Edges defective | 0.009 |
| Edges complete | 0.01 |
| Edges defective + default implant | 0.014 |

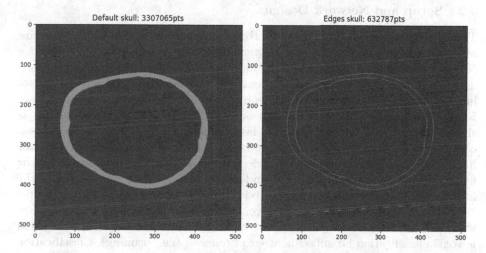

**Fig. 2.** Example of the edge extraction on an axial slice.

**Cropping.** The cropping was mainly driven by a rather low GPU memory availability. The second reason one might consider cropping is that not all parts of the skull scan are equally important for cranial defect reconstruction. The cropping was set to cut away 90 slices of the face, starting from the first non-empty slice and take only $125 + Z \times 0.05$ upper skull slices, where various axial dimensionalities of the provided data are accounted for by the multiplicative factor.

**Subsampling [Optional].** In case of eroding the skull with at least 2 iterations to retain more points or even using the full skull, one can consider randomly taking away 5–8% of the points, while still well preserving the skull geometry and further reducing the input size for SCNN. This type of preprocessing can be considered as pepper noise and can also be used to increase the robustness of the network.

**Implant Extraction.** Once the network reconstructed the skull, we have to extract the implant. For this we subtract the input skull edges from the reconstruction. Postprocessing of the implant involves morphological opening operation with one iteration to reduce residual noise and break thin connections between components, after which the largest connected component (usually the implant) is extracted:

$$Implant = LargestCC(\circ(S_r - S_e)) \tag{3}$$

$\circ$ is the morphological opening operation.

## 3.2   Setup and Network Design

The network is implemented using PyTorch wrapper for Minkowski Engine running on a machine with an AMD Ryzen 7 4800H processor at 3,2 GHz, one Nvidia GeForce RTX 2060 6 GB GPU and 16 GB of DDR4 RAM. The proposed network represents a supervised autoencoder and is comprised of seven convolutional layers for encoding and the same number of layers for decoding (see Fig. 3). An example of encoding layer is shown in Table 2. A decoding layer is similar, except that the convolutional layer is changed to generative transposed convolutional layer. The first encoding layer has a kernel size of 3 and does not have additional convolution. The first decoding layer has a kernel size of 4 for the first transposed convolution. At the end of the network path, the output of the last decoding layer is convolved back to feature dimensionality of 1 with a kernel size of 1 and passed to the Sigmoid layer, which outputs the final skull. The forward pass consists of two paths, where one is for the main features, the second is voxel classification for subsequent voxel removal (i.e., pruning). Classification represents a convolution with kernel size of 1 after each decoding layer to feature dimensionality of 1. The supervision in this case happens for the classification path. The decoding part of the path is a sequence of upsampling and redundant voxel removal, this sequence goes on until the input fidelity level is achieved.

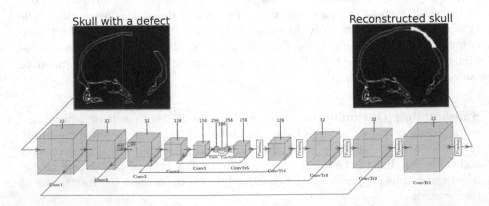

**Fig. 3.** Network architecture (illustration adapted from authors of [6]).

**Table 2.** Encoding layer example

| Layer type | Params |
|---|---|
| Encoding layer | [22 → 32] |
| Convolutional layer | [22 → 32] kernel size = 2 |
| Batch Normalization | - |
| ReLU | - |
| Convolutional layer | [32 → 32] kernel size = 3 |
| Batch Normalization | - |
| ReLU | - |

### 3.3 Training Configuration

The proposed network is a supervised autoencoder, where binary cross entropy loss is minimized by Adam optimizer with the learning rate of 1e–3. From 100 skulls in the provided dataset, 96 were used for training and 4 for evaluation. Batch size was set to 1. The skulls from the training dataset were randomly sampled. To employ a light form of data augmentation, the skulls were mirrored along x-axis with the probability of 0.5. The network contains $1.8 \times 10^7$ parameters and was trained for 16 epochs, which took approximately 2 h. During training, alongside with the input, the ground truth was additionally supplied to the network to supervise the output of the decoding layers and additionally support the pruning process. After each generative transposed convolution, a convolution with the kernel size of 1 is applied to determine which coordinates shall remain and which shall be pruned. This way the network learns to preserve only correct voxels.

### 3.4 Testing Configuration

Evaluation is ommitted for the first epoch, since pruning is not stable enough, which may well result in producing an empty tensor. When evaluating, the target is available, but has no influence over the inference process and serves for evaluation purposes only. Note that since the target does not support the pruning process during evaluation, the evaluation loss is likely to be higher than otherwise expected. When testing on the test set, the target is unavailable and therefore the target is completely ignored during inference.

## 4    Results

This section discusses the results of the network's completion accuracy as well as provides some observations on network's behavior.

## 4.1  Evaluation Metrics

To estimate the quality of the implant prediction on the test set, four metrics were used: Dice Score, Border Dice Score, Hausdorff Distance (HD) and 95th percentile Hausdorff Distance. Border Dice Score here measures how well the predicted implant fits with the borders of the defective skull.

As can be seen in Fig. 5, both Dice and Hausdorff metrics start at reasonable values from the first epoch and only ever slightly improve for the validation set. The network starts with a better Border Dice score, because the pruning layers have not yet learned enough to preserve far lying features well. Note that the validation set of size four contains one extreme case, that drags the metrics towards worse values.

The proposed network performed on the test set fairly well (see Fig. 4), although some outliers are clearly noticeable (see Fig. 6). One main source of such bad performing examples is an underestimation of points in far lying regions. In extreme cases such underestimation might result in no points generated (see Fig. 9). Table 3 shows a quantitative comparison between SCNN and a dense CNN implementation [3] regarding the dice score and HD. We can see that SCNN achieves comparable results with the dense CNN. Note that the SCNN used for experimentation here has roughly 18 million parameters while the dense CNN use two networks with about 85 million and 0.65 million parameters each [1]. Both networks run on 6 GB GPUs. However, the dense CNN requires downsampling and cropping (e.g., bounding box) of the skull images while the sparse CNN can take as input the entire skull image, which well preserves the skull geometry and prevents loss of information.

**Table 3.** Test set performance

| Metric | SCNN | baseline [3] |
|---|---|---|
| Dice score | 0.854 | 0.856 |
| Border dice score | 0.946 | - |
| HD | 4.915 | 5.183 |
| HD95 | 2.645 | - |

## 4.2  Memory Consumption

It was established that initial weight distribution and training samples order play significant role when balancing between the number of input points and memory utilization.

**Weights Initialization.** During the first iteration the weights are initialized randomly, thus the number of generated points is likewise mostly random, which is likely to cause Out Of Memory (OOM) state in memory constrained setups. As can be seen in a possible scenario in Fig. 7, the weight initialization may

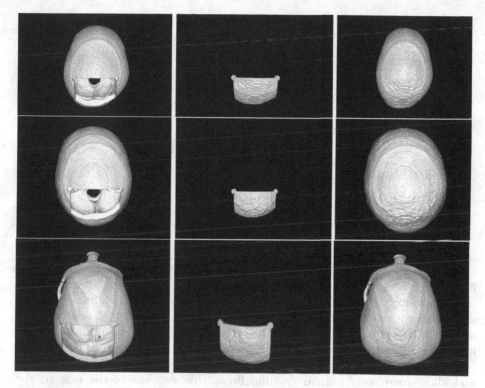

**Fig. 4.** Examples of test set skull reconstruction. The first to the last column show the defective skulls, reconstructed cranial implants and the reconstructed complete skulls, respectively.

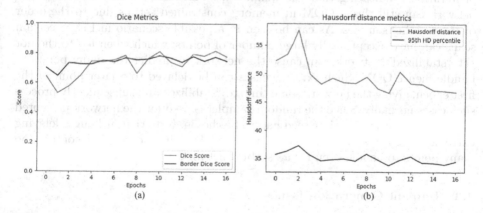

**Fig. 5.** Dice (a) and Hausdorff (b) metrics during training on the validation dataset.

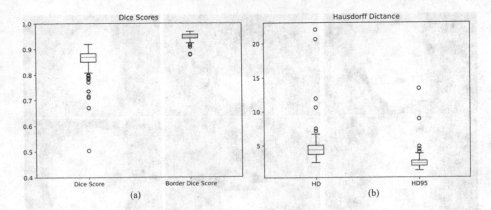

**Fig. 6.** Boxplots of test metrics. A couple of outliers are especially extreme.

cause the network to start with too many points and although the number of predicted points would still converge towards acceptable values, we will not see this happening, as an OOM error will be thrown out immediately. Such behavior may be deceptive at first encounter, because when the network with relatively low number of parameters throws out the OOM error, the user may think that the network is too complex, while in reality changing e.g., a feature dimensionality of some layer to a slightly higher value can positively affect the weight initialization and allow completely normal training flow. This was one of the reasons the presented network has somewhat non-standard feature dimensions.

**Training Samples Order.** Once the network can run past the first couple of iterations, indicating that the weights were initialised rather favorably, the network can still throw OOM in memory constrained setups due to the order of the training samples. As can be seen in a possible scenario in Fig. 8, certain scans can have exceptionally large number of points, which when fed to the not yet "stabilized" network, can cause the network to predict too many points to handle, hence OOM. Such extreme cases can be delayed to a later point of the first epoch, giving the network some time to "stabilize" and subsequently process such cases normally. Since the random sampler is used for the network presented in this work, the appropriate seed had to be chosen. Note that although delaying extreme cases helps in certain cases, there might still be cases that contain too many points to handle even for a "stable" network.

### 4.3 Implant Generation Issues

Upon taking a closer look at the results, it is noticeable that the network tends to underestimate the implant voxels that are relatively far from the defect's edges. This is the main reason of low Dice Scores compared to the Border Dice Scores. In the most extreme case (Fig. 9) only edges could be reconstructed somewhat correctly. One of possible reasons for it might be insufficient amount training

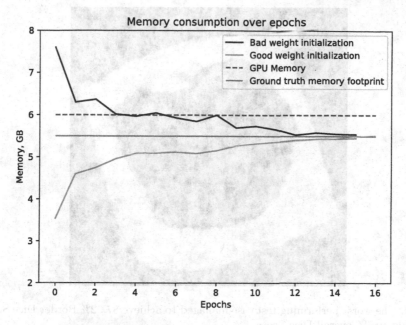

**Fig. 7.** An example of weights initialization importance for illustrative purposes. Unfavorable weight initialization can trigger OOM at the first iteration.

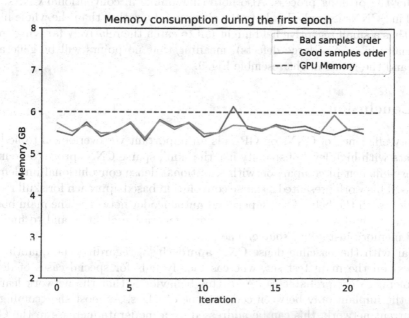

**Fig. 8.** An example of samples order importance for illustrative purposes. Delaying large inputs can help avoid OOM in the first epoch by giving the network more time to stabilize.

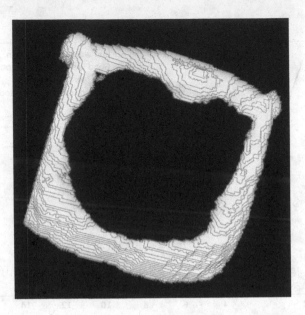

**Fig. 9.** The worst performing test case managed to achieve 87.92% Border Dice Score, but only 50.4% overall Dice Score.

data for the pruning process. Also note that unlike in conventional CNNs, the kernel in SCNNs is applied only to the given points, rather than the whole input data, thus a small receptive field might fail to catch the relatively far lying space (especially in case of large defects), meaning that no points will be generated there and the result might resemble Fig. 9.

## 5   Conclusion

Memory efficiency of CNNs on GPUs is an important yet overlooked topic [10]. For data with high level of sparsity like the skull, sparse CNNs prove to be more memory-efficient in comparison with traditional dense convolutional implementations. This work presented a sparse convolution based approach for skull reconstruction with the help of the supervised autoencoder network. The main obstacles were to find a suitable framework with generative abilities and to find the initial memory instability source. The proposed model shows acceptable results (on par with the baseline dense CNN approach [3] regarding the quantitative metrics) on the main test set, whereas mostly fails for special cases of defect placements. Most probable cause for this behavior is that the network learned to fill the implant only between certain type of edges. As most shortcomings of the current network, this can be addressed by a moderate increase in the GPU memory, as once the network is loaded, the GPU has only 80–75% of 6 GB memory left for dynamic allocations. With more GPU memory available, feeding the full skull can force the network to learn the whole skull structure, rather than the combination of defect skull edges and dense implant. Note, that memory usage of sparse CNNs is linear to the number of points, meaning that a moderate increase in GPU memory could allow processing considerably more points. For example, when training on CPU with 16 GB of RAM using cropped dense skull representation ($5\times$ as many input points), the RAM usage remains below 11 GB (of which Ubuntu host consumes approx. 2 GB), which when "stabilized", becomes roughly 9 GB of RAM. Training on CPU, however, takes up to $30\times$ longer per iteration once the training samples are cached, which makes experiments and hyperparameter tuning unfeasible. That is the reason the proposed network was designed, trained, optimized and tested with 6 GB GPU in focus. Having that mentioned, conventional CNNs require significant downsampling of the volume to run a network even on more advanced GPUs, thus dramatically reducing the number of points and losing some information of the skull structure. The primary goal of this work was to show the ability of sparse networks to reconstruct the skull in its full resolution, that is, to preserve the original skull's geometry and avoid any distortions that could be introduced by both downsampling and upsampling steps. The proposed network based on Minkowski Engine proved to be a good alternative to conventional CNNs, as it allows using the original $512 \times 512 \times Z$ resolution, while being fast and having an acceptable memory footprint. Nonetheless, one should still keep in mind, that the network operates on sparse tensors and the loss calculation is not as trivial as a simple conversion back to the dense tensor. This work was the first approach to the topic of sparse CNN application for skull reconstruction and there are many things to improve in the following work. Here are some options to improve the network's performance:

1. Enrich and/or augment the training dataset with new defects.
2. Consider more points or even the full skull.
3. Landmark detection and subsequent skull transformation proposed in [11] can help both regularize the inputs and considerably decrease the number of input points.
4. Shape priors proposed in [12] might help mitigate the issue of bad performance on large defects.
5. Introduce new loss function capable of further stimulating the generative process of the network to address the underestimation.

**Acknowledgement.** This work was supported by the following funding agencies:
- CAMed (COMET K Project 871132, see also https://www.medunigraz.at/camed/), which is funded by the Austrian Federal Ministry of Transport, Innovation and Technology (BMVIT) and the Austrian Federal Ministry for Digital and Economic Affairs (BMDW), and the Styrian Business Promotion Agency (SFG);
- The Austrian Science Fund (FWF) KLI 678-B31 (enFaced).

# References

1. Li, J., et al.: Autoimplant 2020-first miccai challenge on automatic cranial implant design. IEEE Trans. Med. Imag. **40**, 2329–2342 (2021)

2. Li, J., et al.: Automatic skull defect restoration and cranial implant generation for cranioplasty. Med. Image Anal. **73**, 102171 (2021)
3. Li, J., Pepe, A., Gsaxner, C., Campe, G., Egger, J.: A baseline approach for AutoImplant: the MICCAI 2020 cranial implant design challenge. In: Syeda-Mahmood, T., et al. (eds.) CLIP/ML-CDS -2020. LNCS, vol. 12445, pp. 75–84. Springer, Cham (2020). https://doi.org/10.1007/978-3-030-60946-7_8
4. Li, J., Pepe, A., Gsaxner, C., Jin, Y., Egger, J.: Learning to rearrange voxels in binary segmentation masks for smooth manifold triangulation. arXiv preprint arXiv:2108.05269 (2021)
5. Liu, B., Wang, M., Foroosh, H., Tappen, M., Pensky, M.: Sparse convolutional neural networks. In: Proceedings of the IEEE Conference on Computer Vision and Pattern Recognition, pp. 806–814 (2015)
6. Choy, C., Gwak, J., Savarese, S.: 4D Spatio-temporal convnets: Minkowski convolutional neural networks. In: Proceedings of the IEEE Conference on Computer Vision and Pattern Recognition, pp. 3075–3084 (2019)
7. Li, J., Egger, J.: Dataset descriptor for the AutoImplant cranial implant design challenge. In: Li, J., Egger, J. (eds.) AutoImplant 2020. LNCS, vol. 12439, pp. 10–15. Springer, Cham (2020). https://doi.org/10.1007/978-3-030-64327-0_2
8. Graham, B., van der Maaten, L.: Submanifold sparse convolutional networks. arXiv preprint arXiv:1706.01307 (2017)
9. Gwak, J., Choy, C.B., Savarese, S.: Generative sparse detection networks for 3D single-shot object detection. In: European Conference on Computer Vision (2020)
10. Li, C., Yang, Y., Feng, M., Chakradhar, S., Zhou, H.: Optimizing memory efficiency for deep convolutional neural networks on GPUs. In: SC'16: Proceedings of the International Conference for High Performance Computing, Networking, Storage and Analysis, pp. 633–644. IEEE (2016)
11. Kodym, O., Španěl, M., Herout, A.: Cranial defect reconstruction using cascaded CNN with alignment (2020)
12. Matzkin, E., Newcombe, V., Glocker, B., Ferrante, E.: Cranial implant design via virtual craniectomy with shape prior (2020)

# Cranial Implant Prediction by Learning an Ensemble of Slice-Based Skull Completion Networks

Bokai Yang⬥, Ke Fang⬥, and Xingyu Li(✉)⬥

University of Alberta, Edmonton, AB T6G 2R3, Canada
{bokai5,kfang1,xingyu}@ualberta.ca

**Abstract.** The development of automatic skull reconstruction methods has dramatically reduced the time and expense to repair skull defects. In this study, an ensemble-learning-based method is proposed for skull implant prediction. To overcome the potential overfit problem in 3-D volume analysis using deep learning, a set of 2-D defective skull images is generated by slicing 3-D volumes along the X, Y, and Z axes. We further introduce an RNN model in this method to compensate for the loss of global skull information in the 2-D implant prediction. Over the implant estimation problem in Task 1 of the AutoImplant 2021 challenge, we observe a considerable performance boost from our averaging ensemble strategy and noise removal filtering. The codes for our method as well as our pretrained models is accessible with https://github.com/YouJianFengXue/Cranial-implant-prediction-by-learning-an-ensemble-of-slice-based-skull-completion-networks.

**Keywords:** Cranial implant design · Deep learning · AutoImplant

## 1 Introduction

Defects on cranial bones are usually caused by physical damage or pathological damage to the skulls. Cranioplasty is reconstructive surgery for such skull injury repair. Traditionally, doctors put universal covers on the defective region. However, this solution results in poor aesthetic outcomes and the gap between a skull and implant may not be fully recovered [12]. Later, customized implants were designed to improve the overall cranioplasty outcomes. Patient-specific skull implant customization is a complex procedure with a relatively long waiting time and requires a dedicated CAD software [1,2,7,10]. Recently, there has been an increasing interest in artificial patient-specific implants (PSI). PSI uses computer-aided algorithms and machine learning to generate skull implants based on medical imaging of skull defects and is expected to reduce overall patient risk and surgery time in the operating room [5]. A typical example of PSI is the AutoImplant 2020 challenge, where challenging participants present various data-driven solutions based on triplet of cranial defects and corresponding skull implants. For instance,

© Springer Nature Switzerland AG 2021
J. Li and J. Egger (Eds.): AutoImplant 2021, LNCS 13123, pp. 95–104, 2021.
https://doi.org/10.1007/978-3-030-92652-6_8

classical statistical models such as the statistical shape model (SSM) [8] were used to estimate the skull shape for implant design. We notice that deep learning is still the major technique adopted in this challenge. Specifically, Generative Adversarial Networks (GAN) [8], Variational Autoencoders (VAE) [13], U-Net [3, 4, 6, 9] and its variants, are the most popular generative models for skull completion and implant estimation.

For the purpose of PSI, a defective skull is usually scanned into a 3-D skull volume for downstream analysis. Intuitively, a 3-D U-Net is the candidate network to process the data volume for defective skull recovery. However, this network has many trainable parameters that require a large data set for model training. For one thing, collecting an extensive skull defect data set is expensive. For another, processing a batch of 3-D volumes involves data-intensive computation, which challenges computing resources, especially the memory of a graphic card. We present a hardware-friendly solution to skull implant prediction to address the above issues. Notably, we mitigate the data scarcity issue in model training by slicing the skull volumes into 2-D planes along X, Y, and Z axes for 2-D implant prediction. Simultaneously, the 2-D data analysis and subsequent model ensemble help to reduce the demand on computing hardware.

## 2    Methodology

### 2.1    Dataset

AutoImplant 2021 Challenge is an update of the AutoImplant 2020 Challenge. Particularly for Task 1: cranial implant design for diverse synthetic defects on aligned skulls, 570 cases that are distributed into 5 folders depending on defects' locations are available for training and 100 samples in total (i.e. 20 in each folder) for evaluation. For each training case, a triplet of defective skulls, corresponding complete skull and implant are provided. All data samples are represented in binary $512 \times 512 \times 512$ volumes and saved in NRRD format.

### 2.2    Motivation

3-D skull volume analysis is challenging. Training a 3-D deep model such as the 3-D U-Net on limited samples is prone to overfit, harming models' generalizability on unseen data. In the AutoImplant 2020 Challenge, Shi et al. [11] present a multi-axis slicing solution to address the issue. The method first exploits a 2D CNN network for skull implant estimation on each 2-D plane. Then the obtained skull implant slices are combined to form the final 3-D implant. This algorithm greatly mitigates the requirement of the number of data and computing resources. However, it completely abandons the global information on a skull volume in skull implant perdition. We argue that such global information, especially the continuity between adjacent skull slices, is vital for cranial defect recovery, and considering it in implant design would improve the final results. In this regard, we design an LSTM model to account for the continuity between skull slices; furthermore, we adopt ensemble learning to fuse the outcome of our RNN model and the CNN multiaxial slice network proposed by Shi et al. [11] for final estimation.

## 2.3  Architecture

Figure 1 depicts the diagram of our networks. Given a 3-D defective skull volume, we generate three sets of 2-D planes along the X, Y, and Z axes, respectively. For each slice set, we train two 2-D networks for implant prediction. The CNN model estimates the implant from a single slice, and the RNN neural network takes five continuous slices as its input instead. Before the synthesis step, the system generates six 3-D implant volumes from the parallel processing of the three sets of skull slices. Finally, we combine all six outcomes together by an averaging ensemble strategy. In addition, we design two computational-efficient filters to remove isolated noise for the final output.

Specifically, to prepare 2-D images for downstream CNN and RNN models, a skull volume sample is sliced along X, Y, and Z axis. To decrease the training complexity, we remove the blank slices from the 2-D training sets. Here, blank slices are defined as the images that don't contain skull defect region or cranial bones.

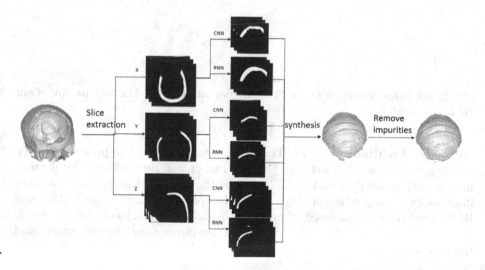

**Fig. 1.** Diagram of our skull implant estimation model. Given a 3-D defective skull volume, we follow the multiaxial slice network proposed by Shi et al. [11] and slice the volumes into 3 sets of 2-D planes. We design an ensemble solution that fuses the CNN and RNN outcomes for final implant prediction. The specific neural network architectures of the CNN and RNN models as well as the data flow in our RNN model are presented in Fig. 2 and Fig. 3, respectively.

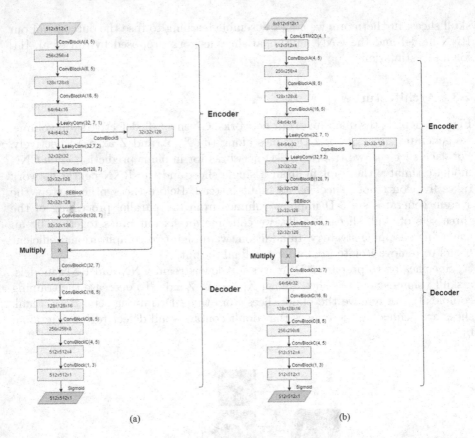

(a)                                    (b)

**Fig. 2.** (a) The architecture of our 2D CNN network and (b) The architecture of our 2D RNN model.

**Network Architecture and Training.** Our solution comprises two deep learning models: a CNN network that focuses on the processing of local information within one slice and an RNN model that takes advantage of continuity information among adjacent slices for skull implant prediction. Both CNN and RNN networks are composed of an encoder and a decoder, as shown in Fig. 2. The encoder projects the 2-D slices into a low-dimensional feature space, and the decoder predicts the skull implant accordingly.

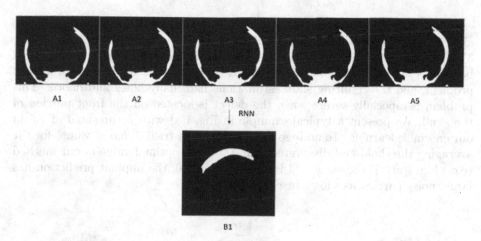

**Fig. 3.** Data flow of the RNN model. A1 to A5 represent the 5 continuous skull slices fed to the RNN model. The slice represented by B1 is the output of the RNN and is treated as the correspond implant of A3 in this study.

Specifically, our CNN model follows the design of the multi-axis study. The RNN model in this study adopts an LSTM module as the first layer above the CNN net, targetting to address the continuity information between adjacent slices for implant prediction. As demonstrated in Fig. 3, a 2-D skull implant is estimated based on five consecutive 2-D slices in the RNN model. To train both networks, we cast the 2-D skull implant estimation problem into a 2-D segmentation problem, where the skull defect is treated as the targeted segmentation region in a skull slice. Therefore, following the conventional segmentation setting, the DICE loss is taken as the objective function for model optimization.

$$Dice\ loss = 1 - \frac{2\Sigma_i \left| P_i * G_i \right| + \xi}{\Sigma_i \left( P_i \right)^2 + \Sigma_j \left( G_j \right)^2 + \xi},\tag{1}$$

where $P_i$ and $G_i$ represent the implant prediction and corresponding ground truth at the pixel $i$, respectively and $\xi$ is a smooth factor to prevent the gradient vanishing or explosion. In this study, we set $\xi = 10^{-6}$.

When we train the models, we use the Adam optimizer with a learning rate of 0.00005 and a clipnorm of 1.0. Due to the limitation of the computing resource, we set the batch size to be 1 during training.

**Implant Synthesis.** With the RNN and CNN models, we obtain six volumes of skull implants, each consisting of all 2-D skull estimations along either X, Y, or Z axes. Then we utilize an ensemble learning strategy to synthesize the final skull implant from the six candidates. Specifically, in both RNN and CNN models, each point in the volume is associated with a probability value indicating the likelihood of a point belonging to the implant. We compare the sum of the six likelihood values to a predefined threshold to determine if the point contributes to the final implant synthesis. In the solution proposed by Shi et al. [11], since only three coarse skull implants are generated, 1.5 (i.e., 0.5 × 3) is taken as the threshold to differentiate the defective region and cranial bone in a 3D volume. However, we found this threshold inappropriate for our problem, and the resulting skull estimations had many holes and debris. This problem is especially severe when the defect is located on the front portion of the skull. We present a typical example in Fig. 4(a) with a threshold of 1.5 in our ensemble learning. To address this problem, we tried different values for the averaging threshold and discovered that 1.0 is the optimal value in our method (e.g., Fig. 4(c)). If the threshold is smaller than 1.0, the implant prediction has large, noisy parties, as shown in Fig. 4(b)).

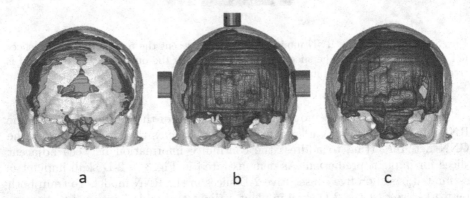

a                    b                    c

**Fig. 4.** Different threshold versus skull synthesis from the six coarse defect volumes. (a) Threshold of 1.5 (b) threshold of 0.5, and (c) threshold of 1.0. The grey regions correspond to defective skull and the red ones represent skull implants generated under different thresholds.

**Impurity Filter.** In skull synthesis, we observe small, isolated artifacts outside of skulls. Therefore, we design two simple filters to remove the isolated noise in the predicted implants, one in the dimension of $7 \times 7 \times 7$ and the other in $11 \times 11 \times 11$. Please refer to the Experiment and Result section for the qualitative and quantitative evaluation of the ensemble strategy and impurity filters.

## 3    Experimentation and Results

After training our networks using provided training samples, we submit the predicted implants to the challenge organizer and get feedback on the quantitative evaluation. In this problem, 3 metrics including Hausdorff distance (HD) and dice similarity score (DSC), and broader dice are used for performance assessment.

Since our method has extensive overlap with the solution proposed by Shi et al. [11], we downloaded their Github code, run their model on the Task 1 data in this challenge from scratch, and took it as our comparison baseline in this study. The statistics over the test set are presented in Table 1, where all numerical metrics are averaged over the five folders. The specific quantitative evaluation results over the five folders are presented in the Appendix. As we explained and reported in the Appendix, our submission of the baseline model had unexpected errors on the test samples in the folder of random2. So we report two sets of results for the baseline model, where the numerical values associated with "Baseline" in the first row are computed from the results of the first four folders in Table 2 and the values in the second row marked as "Baseline*" are averaged over evaluations across all 5 folders for your reference. The results in Table 1 suggest that both our ensemble learning strategy and the impurity filters improve the implant prediction performance. To visualize the performance boost obtained by our ensemble strategy, we present two skull implant predictions in Fig. 5 for comparison. Skull implants in the first row are predicted by the baseline CNN network only, and the examples in the second row are generated after our averaging ensemble strategy. From the figure, the implants in the first row are incomplete. After our ensemble strategy to combine CNN and RNN results, the implants in the second two are complete with more smooth surfaces.

**Table 1.** The comparison of DICE, border DICE, and HD95 among the baseline model, ensemble learning model, and our final solutions.

|                          | HD95  | DICE | Border DICE |
|--------------------------|-------|------|-------------|
| Baseline                 | 3.09  | 0.77 | 0.81        |
| Baseline*                | 16.74 | 0.64 | 0.68        |
| CNN+RNN                  | 7.47  | 0.80 | 0.85        |
| CNN+RNN+Impurity filter  | 3.33  | 0.81 | 0.86        |

In the future, we would like to improve this method in the following two directions. First, this method includes two simple filters to remove small unwanted parties from the synthesis implant. However, the two filters are incapable of eliminating large impurities. We want to utilize connected component analysis to remove isolated noise. Second, this study explores RNN quite naively (i.e., adding an LSTM layer on the top of a CNN model). We believe that training an entirely new RNN model from scratch will improve the overall performance.

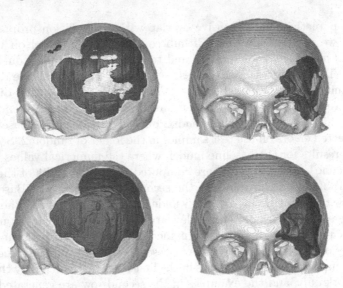

**Fig. 5.** This figure shows the effect of ensemble learning. Skull implants in the first row are predicted by the CNN network only and the examples in the second row are generated by our method. The implants in the first row have holes on the surface. After our ensemble strategy to combine CNN and RNN results together, the implants in the second row are both improved with more smooth and complete surfaces.

## 4    Conclusions

This paper proposed a new skull implant design method by inpainting defective regions in 2-D skull slices. Since the networks take 2-D images/planes as the input, the models had fewer trainable parameters and thus mitigated the negative effects of a limited number of training samples. The quantitative and qualitative results indicated that our averaging ensemble strategy over coarse implants and the two purity filters helped improve the performance.

## Appendix

In this challenge, we made several submissions for algorithm assessment and improvement. The specific quantitative evaluation of our submissions that comes from the challenge organizer are presented in this section. Specifically, Table 2 reports the performance of the baseline CNN model on the test samples in the five folders. Note that our submission encountered unexpected errors over the test samples in the folder of random2. So we particularly include this information here for your reference or any further research and report the performance of the baseline through two sets of numerical values in Table 1, where the values in the first row are computed from the results of the first four folders and the second line corresponds to the performance assessment over all 5 folders. We believe that quantitative measurement in the first row of Table 1 reflects the the performance of our baseline model. Similarly, Table 3 and Table 4 report the specific numerical results for our later submissions. Slightly different from the baseline model, the final results presented in Table 1 are averaged over the five folders.

**Table 2.** The quantitative results of the baseline network from the challenge organizer. Note that our submission had unexpected errors on the test samples in the folder of random2. So we faithfully mark the error here with the star sign $*$ for your reference.

|             | Bilateral | Frontoorbital | Parietotemporal | Random1 | Random2 |
|-------------|-----------|---------------|-----------------|---------|---------|
| DICE        | 0.74      | 0.76          | 0.80            | 0.79    | 0.11*   |
| Border DICE | 0.80      | 0.79          | 0.86            | 0.82    | 0.10*   |
| HD95        | 4.06      | 2.84          | 2.44            | 3.04    | 71.32*  |

**Table 3.** The quantitative results of the our CNN+RNN models from the challenge organizer.

|             | Bilateral | Frontoorbital | Parietotemporal | Random1 | Random2 |
|-------------|-----------|---------------|-----------------|---------|---------|
| DICE        | 0.79      | 0.80          | 0.83            | 0.80    | 0.79    |
| Border DICE | 0.84      | 0.82          | 0.88            | 0.84    | 0.84    |
| HD95        | 10.56     | 8.70          | 2.64            | 7.60    | 7.85    |

**Table 4.** The quantitative evaluation of the entire solution from the challenge organizer.

|             | Bilateral | Frontoorbital | Parietotemporal | Random1 | Random2 |
|-------------|-----------|---------------|-----------------|---------|---------|
| DICE        | 0.80      | 0.81          | 0.84            | 0.80    | 0.80    |
| Border DICE | 0.85      | 0.83          | 0.89            | 0.86    | 0.85    |
| HD95        | 3.87      | 2.70          | 2.63            | 3.87    | 3.60    |

# References

1. Chen, X., Xu, L., Li, X., Egger, J.: Computer-aided implant design for the restoration of cranial defects. Sci. Rep. **7**, 4199 (2017)
2. Dean, D., Min, K.-J.: Computer aided design of cranial implants using deformable templates (2003)
3. Ellis, D.G., Aizenberg, M.R.: Deep learning using augmentation via registration: 1st place solution to the AutoImplant 2020 challenge. In: Li, J., Egger, J. (eds.) AutoImplant 2020. LNCS, vol. 12439, pp. 47–55. Springer, Cham (2020). https://doi.org/10.1007/978-3-030-64327-0_6

4. Ellis, D.G., Aizenberg, M.R.: Deep learning using augmentation via registration: 1st place solution to the AutoImplant 2020 challenge. In: Li, J., Egger, J. (eds.) AutoImplant 2020. LNCS, vol. 12439, pp. 47–55. Springer, Cham (2020). https://doi.org/10.1007/978-3-030-64327-0_6

5. Li, J., et al.: Towards the automatization of cranial implant design in cranioplasty: 2nd MICCAI Challenge on Automatic Cranial Implant Design, March 2021. https://doi.org/10.1007/978-3-030-64327-0

6. Mainprize, J.G., Fishman, Z., Hardisty, M.R.: Shape completion by U-Net: an approach to the AutoImplant MICCAI cranial implant design challenge. In: Li, J., Egger, J. (eds.) AutoImplant 2020. LNCS, vol. 12439, pp. 65–76. Springer, Cham (2020). https://doi.org/10.1007/978-3-030-64327-0_8

7. Ming-Yih, L., Chong-Ching, C., Chao-Chun, L., Lun-Jou, L., Yu-Ray, C.: Custom implant design for patients with cranial defects. IEEE Eng. Med. Biol. Mag. **21**, 38–44 (2002)

8. Pimentel, P., et al.: Automated virtual reconstruction of large skull defects using statistical shape models and generative adversarial networks. In: Li, J., Egger, J. (eds.) AutoImplant 2020. LNCS, vol. 12439, pp. 16–27. Springer, Cham (2020). https://doi.org/10.1007/978-3-030-64327-0_3

9. Eder, M., Li, J., Egger, J.: Learning volumetric shape super-resolution for cranial implant design. In: Li, J., Egger, J. (eds.) AutoImplant 2020. LNCS, vol. 12439, pp. 104–113. Springer, Cham (2020). https://doi.org/10.1007/978-3-030-64327-0_12

10. Scharver, C., Evenhouse, R., Johnson, A., Leigh, J.: Pre-surgical cranial implant design using the Paris/SPL trade/prototype. IEEE Virtual Real. **2004**, 199–291 (2004)

11. Shi, H., Chen, X.: Cranial implant design through multiaxial slice inpainting using deep learning. In: Li, J., Egger, J. (eds.) AutoImplant 2020. LNCS, vol. 12439, pp. 28–36. Springer, Cham (2020). https://doi.org/10.1007/978-3-030-64327-0_4

12. Gord von Campe and Karin Pistracher. Patient specific implants (PSI) cranioplasty in the neurosurgical clinical routine. In: AutoImplant 2020, LNCS 12439, pp. 1–9, 2020 (2020)

13. Wang, B., et al.: Cranial implant design using a deep learning method with anatomical regularization. In: Li, J., Egger, J. (eds.) AutoImplant 2020. LNCS, vol. 12439, pp. 85–93. Springer, Cham (2020). https://doi.org/10.1007/978-3-030-64327-0_10

# PCA-Skull: 3D Skull Shape Modelling Using Principal Component Analysis

Lei Yu[1,2], Jianning Li[1,2,3], and Jan Egger[1,2,3]($\boxtimes$)

[1] Institute of Computer Graphics and Vision, Graz University of Technology,
Inffeldgasse 16, 8010 Graz, Austria
{jianning.li,egger}@icg.tugraz.at
[2] Computer Algorithms for Medicine Laboratory (Café-Lab), 8010 Graz, Austria
[3] Institute for AI in Medicine (IKIM), University Hospital Essen, Girardetstraße 2,
45131 Essen, Germany

**Abstract.** Cranial implant design is aimed to repair skull defects caused by brain related diseases like brain tumor and high intracranial pressure. Researches have found that deep neural networks could potentially help accelerate the design procedure and get better results. However, most algorithms fail to handle the generalization problem: deep learning models are expected to generalize well to varied defect patterns on high-resolution skull images, while they tend to overfit to some specific defect patterns (shape, location, etc.) in the training set. We employ principle components analysis (PCA) to model the shape of healthy human skulls. We assume that defective skulls have similar shape distributions to healthy skulls in a common principle component (PC) space, as a defect, which usually only occupies a fraction of the whole skull, would not substantially deviate a human skull from its original shape distribution in a compact PC space. Applying inverse PCA to the principal components of defective skulls would therefore yield their healthy counterparts. A subtraction operation between the reconstructed healthy skulls and the defect skulls is followed to obtain the final implants. Our method is evaluated on the datasets of Task 2 and Task 3 of the AutoImplant 2021 challenge (https://autoimplant2021.grand-challenge. org/). Using only 25 healthy skulls to create the PCA model, the method nonetheless shows satisfactory results on both datasets. Results also show the good generalization performance of the proposed PCA-based method for skull shape modelling. Codes can be found at https://github.com/ 1eiyu/ShapePrior.

**Keywords:** Cranioplasty · Shape prior · Modelling · Shape registration · Deep learning · Principal component analysis

## 1 Introduction

The manual reconstruction of complicated defective skulls remains a great challenge at present. It is time-consuming and needs to be carried out by professional designers. Recent advances in deep convolutional neural networks (CNNs)

© Springer Nature Switzerland AG 2021
J. Li and J. Egger (Eds.): AutoImplant 2021, LNCS 13123, pp. 105–115, 2021.
https://doi.org/10.1007/978-3-030-92652-6_9

(CNN) have the potential to free surgeons and designers from complex modelling procedure and expensive computer-aided design (CAD) software.

A baseline CNN solution submitted by the organizers of AutoImplant Cranial Implant Design challenge in 2020 proposed a two-stage method, which localizes the defect area automatically and generates the final implant directly from a bounding box of the defect [1]. However, the results show that the proposed method is not sensitive to the shape of the defects and lack robustness for those out-of-distribution test cases.

Previous studies show that using a shape prior of complete skull is a potentially effective way to improve the generalization ability on the original high-resolution data [2,3]. A shape prior can be used to represent the general shape distribution of an object such as the human skull, which furthermore help ease the over-fitting problems caused by uneven distribution of training sets and improve the reliability of the algorithm. Besides using a shape prior, previous studies also reveal that data augmentation - through either augmenting the defect patterns in the training set [4] or augmenting the skull images [5] could help deep learning models generalize better.

Shape registrations between skull images could allow the alignment of anatomical skull features among a group of complete skulls through transformation operations like translation, scaling and rotation, which further facilitate the extraction of these features. Another advantage of registration is that skull images of difference sizes can be transformed into a common space, where the registered skull images have the same size, which is beneficial for subsequent CNN or non-CNN-based image processing pipelines.

Inspired by previous studies especially by the work from Matzkin et al. [6] and Pimentel et al. [7], we designed a workflow to predict the shape of implants given the original defective skulls. The key ingredient of the workflow is the modelling of human skulls using a principal component analysis (PCA) based method. Limited by the computation capacity, only 25 healthy skulls are used to create a principal component (PC) space, where the general shape distributions of human skulls are captured. The method depicts satisfactory generalization performance on various synthetic defect patterns as well as on real defects from craniotomy.

## 2    Method

This proposed workflow reconstructs the full skull first using PCA, and then the original image can be subtracted from it to generate a difference image i.e., the implant. Registration is first employed for the purpose of aligning the selected complete skulls with a fixed skull. For training, the registered complete skulls are used to create a PC space. For testing, the defective skulls are first registered with the same fixed skull as the training skulls images did and then mapped into the previously built PC space. To generate the corresponding complete skulls for the test cases, an inverse PCA is applied on the principal components of the defective skulls. Note that the generated complete skulls need to be transformed

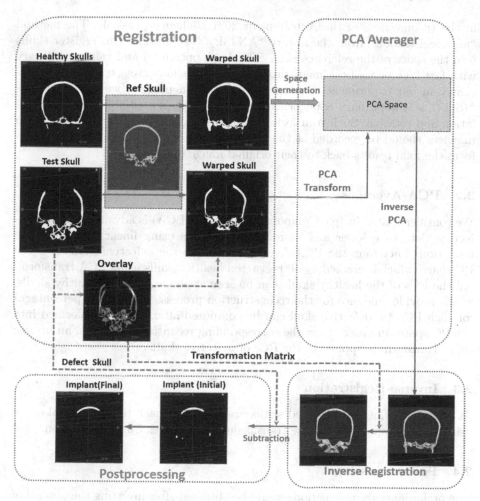

**Fig. 1.** General architecture of PCA-based 3D skull shape modelling and cranial implant generation

back to their original dimension based on the transformation matrix generated in the registration step. The cranial implant can be obtained via a subtraction process. In the last step, we make some post-processing to obtain clean implants without any noise. The workflow is illustrated in Fig. 1.

## 2.1 Registration

We employ a registration method which could align the complete skulls with a pre-selected skull. The aim of registration is to align the anatomical features of the selected skulls and map the varied-sized skulls into a common space. We pre-select a skull image as a reference for registration from the healthy skulls in the training sets of the AutoImplant 2021 challenge (Task 3). The method "ants.registration" from the library "ANTsPy" [8] is utilized to register skulls into the space of the reference skull. This is an optimized and validated library with fast I/O for medical image processing and it shows great computation efficiency in our experiment. During the registration process, we mainly choose "Rigid" as the primary transformation type, which is a combination of translation and rotation. Such transformation and the corresponding transformation matrices should be recorded at the same time of registration in order to transform the final results back to their original image domain.

## 2.2    PCA-Averager

We consider that Principle Components Analysis (PCA) is advantageous to projecting data to a lower and more compact space using linear dimensionality reduction. Therefore, the PCA-Averager can map the defective skulls into the PC space, which is created by all registered healthy skulls using PCA transform. All the PCs of the healthy skulls can be seen as shape priors of healthy skulls, which provide guidance for the reconstruction process. The scores (percentage) for each PC of a defective skull can be computed after being transformed into the PC space. In order to get the corresponding reconstructed skulls, an inverse PCA-Transform is applied to the PCs of defective skulls.

## 2.3    Inverse-Registration

At this stage, the reconstructed skulls are converted back to their initial space using the corresponding inverse transformation matrices from registration.

## 2.4    Post-processing

The preliminary reconstructions would be obtained after inverting the process of registration. We then employ a subtraction operation in order to get the shape of the implants, which would inevitably need to be denoised via post-processing. First, the connected components analysis in the *python* package "cc3d" helps us label each connected component in the implant images. Then we simply apply an "opening" morphological operation to the implants. There is a trade-off between different choices of opening radius: large value results in marginal information losses of implant, while smaller value fails to remove some artifacts connected to the implant. For images on which the artifacts are difficult to remove, we try different radius parameters for the opening operation and then make a simple subtraction between them. The output after this process could be a combination of part of implant to be saved and noise to be removed. Another "cc3d" method can be applied in order to remove these noise and get more accurate prediction.

**Fig. 2.** Example of a triplet training sample: complete skull (left), defective skull (mid), implant (right) from Task 3 of the AutoImplant 2021 challenge.

## 3   Experiment and Results

### 3.1   Dataset

Our project is based on the datasets for the AutoImplant 2021 MICCAI challenge (https://autoimplant2021.grand-challenge.org/). The training set consists of 100 triplets of binary skull data with the same suffix "Nrrd". Each triplet includes a complete skull, a defective skull and its corresponding implant. One example of the triplet can be seen in Fig. 2. Due to limited computation power (1.4 GHz Quad-Core Intel Core i5) and memory size (8 GB 2133 MHz LPDDR3 RAM), we could only choose the first 25 healthy samples as training data. For the test sets of Task 3, the challenge officials also provides 10 extra skulls with different shape, size and location of the defects, apart from the 100 normal test cases. In order to further validate the generalization ability of our method, we also run the test on the Task 2 dataset of the challenge, which contains 11 real defective skulls from clinical operations.

**Table 1.** Mean and standard deviation (Std) of Dice similarity coefficient (DSC), Border Dice similarity coefficient (bDSC) and 95% Hausdorff distances (HD95) for the 11 real clinical cases on the Task 2 dataset

|       | HD95 (mm) | Dice | bDSC |
|-------|-----------|------|------|
| Mean  | 8.35      | 0.51 | 0.45 |
| Std   | 2.54      | 0.12 | 0.10 |

### 3.2   Results on Task 2 of the AutoImplant 2021 Challenge

Table 1 and Fig. 3 show the quantitative results for dice similarity coefficient (DSC), border DSC (bDSC) and 95% hausdorff distance (HD95) on the 11 real

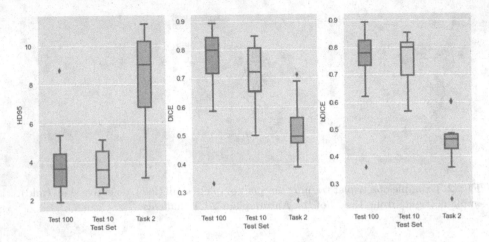

**Fig. 3.** Distribution of Dice similarity coefficient, Border Dice similarity coefficient and Hausdorff distances regards to different test sets (Test 100, Test 10 and Task 2).

craniectomy cases. Note that even if the test data from Task 2 are from a different population compared to the training data, our methods could get a reasonable 50% matching with the ground truth implants in terms of both Dice metrics. Low accuracy may result not only from the small size of training data we used, but also the inherent drawbacks of the method itself. For example, Fig. 4 shows that our method can receive good feedback for test cases with moderate defect sizes like (A), whereas for large defects like (B), our method is suboptimal, considering that for large defects, our assumption that healthy skulls and defective skulls share similar shape distributions in the PC space won't hold. However, it should be noted that the low quantitative scores won't necessarily invalidate the clinical usability of our results, as the ground truth implants are only one of the acceptable solutions [2]. We can see from Fig. 4 that our implants can actually match well with the defects on the defective skulls.

### 3.3   Results on Task 3 of the AutoImplant 2021 Challenge

Table 2 and Fig. 3 show the quantitative results for DSC, bDSC and HD95 on the 100 normal test cases and the 10 extra test cases. We can see that even though the defects in the 10 extra test cases varied greatly from those in the normal test cases (as well as in the 25 training data), our method has stable performance on both datasets in terms of the three metrics, indicating the good generalization ability of the proposed method. Qualitatively, although only 25 complete skulls are used for training, our method can produce implants that match fairly well with the defective skulls from both test sets of Task 3, as can be seen from Fig. 5.

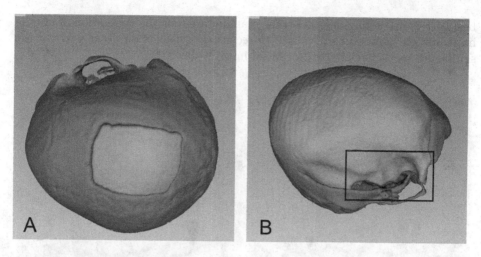

**Fig. 4.** Examples of qualitative results on the Task 2 dataset. (A) shows a good match between a defect and an implant, while (B) fails to predict the lower part of implant due to the large defect area.

**Table 2.** Dice similarity coefficient (DSC), Border Dice similarity coefficient (bDSC) and 95% Hausdorff distances (HD95) for the 100 normal test cases and 10 extra test cases in task 3

|  | HD95 (mm) | Dice | bDSC |
|---|---|---|---|
| 100 normal test cases | 3.68 | 0.78 | 0.77 |
| 10 extra test cases | 3.65 | 0.71 | 0.75 |
| Overall cases | 3.68 | 0.77 | 0.77 |

**Table 3.** Dice similarity coefficient (DSC) copmpared with other methods in task 3 from last year

| Methods | Test 100 cases | Test 10 cases | Overall |
|---|---|---|---|
| Baseline [1] | 0.86 | – | – |
| Matzkin et al. [3] | 0.91 | 0.77 | 0.90 |
| Ours | 0.78 | 0.71 | 0.77 |

## 3.4  Visualization of the Principle Components

Figure 6 shows the visualization of the first two PCs. As we can see, the PC shown in (A) captures the contour of the healthy skulls, while the PC in (B) captures the lower skull part. More importantly, the visualization reveals that, besides reconstructing defects on the cranium area for the generation of cranial implants, our method can be used to reconstruct defects on other parts of the skull, such as the facial area (for facial implant design).

**Fig. 5.** Examples of qualitative results on the 100 normal test cases (first row) and the 10 extra test cases (second row) from Task 3 of the AutoImplant 2021 challenge.

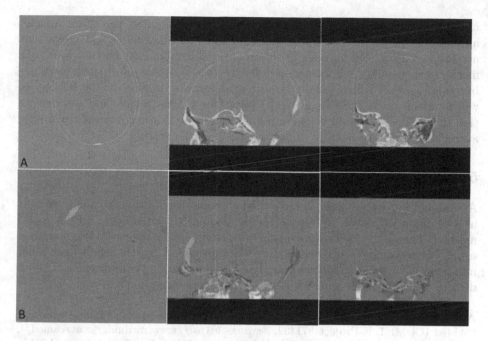

**Fig. 6.** The first two principle components of the healthy skulls. Different PCs capture different features of the skull shape. (A) focused on the skull contour while (B) focused on the lower part of the skull.

## 4    Discussion and Future Work

Out of the 11 methods from AutoImplant 2020, only 6 are able to generalize to the extra 10 test cases. Compared with other methods shown in Table 3, our quantitative and qualitative results look quite satisfactory with only 25 complete skulls as training data. Most importantly, this pca-based solution also succeeds in generalizing to different shapes and positons. In general, the method requires only healthy skulls for training and thus is independent from the shape and position of the skull defects. Besides cranial implant design, our method may be potentially useful for facial implant design as well. However, a few shortcomings still need to be clarified here.

Most defective areas in the test cases appear to be small or medium sized, which can be recovered with sufficient quality using our method. Nevertheless, as shown in Fig. 4(B), our method cannot restore effectively the very large defects. One hypothesis is that large defect area may result in continuous information loss that altered the shape distribution of the skull. Using non-linear registration might help normalize the skulls better prior to principal component analysis. Another limitation of our method is that the number of PCs are limited by the number of training samples (only 25 skulls are used for training), while each 3D skull image has $512 \times 512 \times Z$ features ($Z$ is the number of slices). Therefore, our method may not be capable of extracting local geometric features in details. Furthermore, post-processing is usually required to obtain a clean implant. For different test cases, parameters in the morphological operations need to be customized in order to obtain optimal results. Last but not least, our method can handle skull images of difference sizes[1], unlike most deep learning-based approaches which usually require a uniform input size. In the future, we will focus on using the PCs as shape priors for CNNs in the skull reconstruction task. The PCs could be more robust geometric priors compared to simply averaging a group of healthy skulls as used in earlier studies.

## 5  Conclusion

Assuming that defective skulls have similar shape distributions to healthy skulls in a common PC space, we reconstruct the complete skulls using a PCA-based method. The method shows good generalization performance even when trained using only a quarter of the training data provided by the challenge. Most importantly, our method shows potential in reconstructing complex clinical skull defects, which is challenging for deep learning-based methods.

**Acknowledgement.** This work was supported by the following funding agencies: CAMed (COMET K-Project 871132, see also https://www.medunigraz.at/camed/), which is funded by the Austrian Federal Ministry of Transport, Innovation and Technology (BMVIT) and the Austrian Federal Ministry for Digital and Economic Affairs (BMDW), and the Styrian Business Promotion Agency (SFG); The Austrian Science Fund (FWF) KLI 678-B31 (enFaced).

## References

1. Li, J., Pepe, A., Gsaxner, C., Campe, G., Egger, J.: A baseline approach for AutoImplant: the MICCAI 2020 cranial implant design challenge. In: Syeda-Mahmood, T., et al. (eds.) CLIP/ML-CDS -2020. LNCS, vol. 12445, pp. 75–84. Springer, Cham (2020). https://doi.org/10.1007/978-3-030-60946-7_8
2. Li, J., et al.: AutoImplant 2020-first MICCAI challenge on automatic cranial implant design. IEEE Trans. Med. Imaging **40**(9), 2329–2342 (2021)
3. Matzkin, F., Newcombe, V., Glocker, B., Ferrante, E.: Cranial implant design via virtual craniectomy with shape priors. In: Li, J., Egger, J. (eds.) AutoImplant 2020. LNCS, vol. 12439, pp. 37–46. Springer, Cham (2020). https://doi.org/10.1007/978-3-030-64327-0_5
4. Li, J., et al.: Automatic skull defect restoration and cranial implant generation for cranioplasty. Med. Image Anal. **73**, 102171 (2021)
5. Ellis, D.G., Aizenberg, M.R.: Deep learning using augmentation via registration: 1st place solution to the AutoImplant 2020 challenge. In: Li, J., Egger, J. (eds.) AutoImplant 2020. LNCS, vol. 12439, pp. 47–55. Springer, Cham (2020). https://doi.org/10.1007/978-3-030-64327-0_6
6. Matzkin, F., et al.: Self-supervised skull reconstruction in brain CT images with decompressive craniectomy. In: Martel, A.L. (ed.) MICCAI 2020. LNCS, vol. 12262, pp. 390–399. Springer, Cham (2020). https://doi.org/10.1007/978-3-030-59713-9_38

---

[1] Not all test cases in Task 2 have a size of $512 \times 512 \times Z$.

7. Pimentel, P., et al.: Automated virtual reconstruction of large skull defects using statistical shape models and generative adversarial networks. In: Li, J., Egger, J. (eds.) AutoImplant 2020. LNCS, vol. 12439, pp. 16–27. Springer, Cham (2020). https://doi.org/10.1007/978-3-030-64327-0_3

8. Avants, B.B., Tustison, N., Song, G., et al.: Advanced normalization tools (ANTS). Insight J. **2**(365), 1–35 (2009)

# Cranial Implant Design Using V-Net Based Region of Interest Reconstruction

Shashwat Pathak[1], Chitimireddy Sindhura[1], Rama Krishna Sai S. Gorthi[1], Degala Venkata Kiran[2], and Subrahmanyam Gorthi[1(✉)]

[1] Department of Electrical Engineering, Indian Institute of Technology Tirupati, Tirupati, India
s.gorthi@iittp.ac.in
[2] Department of Mechanical Engineering, Indian Institute of Technology Tirupati, Tirupati, India

**Abstract.** Cranial implant design is a sophisticated time-intensive process performed by specialists uniquely for each patient using a set of standardized cranioplasty procedures. Automating the design of cranial implants for the 'in-Operating-Room' (in-OR) manufacturing pipeline is required to perform cranioplasty immediately after the primary surgery, thereby reducing the overall surgery time. In this manuscript, we propose an efficient cranial implant design workflow through a two-step approach in which we use two V-Net architectures, one to extract the region of cranial defect from the low-resolution skull and the other to reconstruct the cranial defect in the high-resolution skull. The extracted defective cranium is subtracted from the reconstructed cranium and is post-processed to obtain the fine implant. We further performed experiments to manufacture the cranial implant predicted by our proposed method through 3D printing, using titanium-aluminium (Ti6-Al4-V) alloy, a standard material used for medical prosthetics and implants. The proposed method is trained and evaluated on the data provided by the MICCAI 2021 AutoImplant Challenge. Our method performed well, giving a Dice Similarity Coefficient (DSC) of 0.90, border DSC of 0.95, and a 95-percentile of the Hausdorff Distance (HD95) of 2.02 mm over the test dataset (000.nrrd–109.nrrd).

**Keywords:** Cranioplasty · Implant design · Skull reconstruction · Deep learning · 3D printing · V-Net

## 1 Introduction

Cranioplasty is a popular surgical procedure in neurosurgery to cover skull defects by inserting cranial implants made of plastic or metals. The skull defects are mostly caused by injuries leading to cracks or depressions in the skull or medical treatments such as brain tumour operations. In order to restore the shape of the skull and protect the brain from further injuries, it is essential to fill the defects with cranial implants. The design of cranial implants is currently patient-specific and designed using commercially available software with

© Springer Nature Switzerland AG 2021
J. Li and J. Egger (Eds.): AutoImplant 2021, LNCS 13123, pp. 116–128, 2021.
https://doi.org/10.1007/978-3-030-92652-6_10

highly qualified professional clinical experts. This is a very time-consuming process and requires the intervention of many clinical experts from designing to manufacturing. It is essential to develop an automatic cranial implant design technique with high accuracy that could conform well to the boundaries of the defective cranial region. Recent advances in deep learning have paved the way to automate the critical problems in medical imaging, thereby reducing human interventions to a great extent. The various methods used in AutoImplant challenge 2020 outperformed traditional methods in several aspects such as accuracy, computational efficiency, training time, etc. [3,14]. However, there is still scope for further improving the performance in multiple aspects, and that is perhaps the motivation for hosting a second AutoImplant challenge in MICCAI 2021.

There are broadly two ways to design the cranial implants, as shown in Fig. 1. The first approach is the direct generation of implants. The second approach is to predict the whole skull, followed by subtracting the defective skull to get the final implant. Figure 1a and 1b illustrate the above mentioned direct implant prediction approach and subtraction-based reconstruction approach respectively. Among the methods presented at the AutoImplant challenge 2020, only a few are based on direct implant generation [9,16,20].

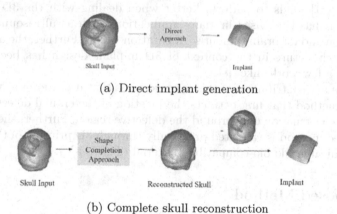

(a) Direct implant generation

(b) Complete skull reconstruction

**Fig. 1.** The flow diagrams of two of the most widely used approaches for cranial implant design.

The direct implant generation approach aims to predict the implant directly. Since the implant is a smaller volume with simple shape properties, it is computationally efficient to predict using deep learning-based approaches. However, the difficulty with the direct implant generation approach illustrated in Fig. 1a is the surface inconsistency around the edges of the implant, predicted by encoder-decoder networks. This inconsistency is due to the model's inability to grasp and accurately reproduce the high-level features around the edges. This leads to a possibility that the implant might not fit appropriately into the defective skull, especially when the defects are more complex, having different shapes.

The complete skull reconstruction approach, as illustrated in Fig. 1b is formulated as a shape completion problem. Even though it tends to fix the edge inconsistency due to subtraction in obtaining the fine implant, it has its challenges. The human skull is a highly sophisticated structure made up of grooves, curved surfaces, and other complex structures, making learning its shape properties computationally intensive. In addition, the mesh size of the entire skull is huge compared to a smaller volume such as the implant in the direct implant generation approach. So, a deep learning model with higher parameters and longer training time is required to achieve good results and accurately predict the shape of the complete skull.

Most of the methods that use the complete skull reconstruction approach tend to use the U-Net [19] architecture and its derivatives. In [2], the skull completion task is performed on scans with low resolution and extrapolated to full resolution. A method based on super-resolution is proposed in [5] whereas a patch-based training method has been suggested in [8]. In [15], the defective skull is cropped as a pre-processing step, and the U-Net [19] model is trained on the cropped defective skulls to output a complete skull, while [21] proposed a U-Net architecture based on residual dense blocks.

Despite U-Net performing well for segmentation in 2D images, it is observed that V-Net [17] tends to perform better when dealing with the 3D data. For instance, this has been used in many applications such as ultrasound prostate segmentation and for brain tumour segmentation [4,11]. Further, the application of V-Net architecture in the context of 3D implant design has been recently explored in a few works like [8].

The primary contribution of this manuscript is that it proposes a two-step V-Net based method that first extracts the location of the cranial defect and then performs reconstruction only around the defective region. Further, the output of the proposed method is validated practically through 3D printing of the implant using a medical-grade bio-compatible material (Ti6-Al4-V).

## 2    Proposed Method

As mentioned in the preceding section, the direct implant generation approach is computationally more efficient than the complete skull reconstruction. However direct implant generation approaches are generally prone to errors around the boundaries of the predicted implant. On the other hand, the complete skull reconstruction followed by subtraction approach provides relatively more accurate implants, and consistency around the edges, but at the cost of higher computational expense. Our proposed method in this paper leverages from the best of both the approaches through a two-stage Region of Interest (RoI) reconstruction model.

The proposed approach to obtain the final implant can be divided into three major steps: (i) defect localization, (ii) defective region extraction, and (iv) implant reconstruction followed by post-processing. These three steps are presented in detail in the following subsections.

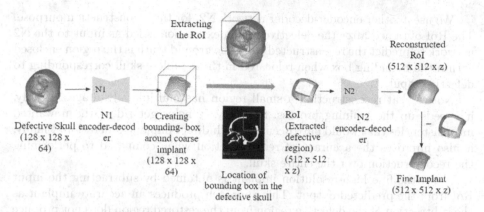

**Fig. 2.** The workflow diagram of the proposed method for cranial implant design

## 2.1 Defect Localization

The defect localization step used in this paper is similar to the approach proposed in [13]. The full resolution skull is scaled down to $128 \times 128 \times 64$ to obtain a coarse skull and is given as an input to the first encoder-decoder network N1 shown in Fig. 2. The output of the N1 network is a coarse implant that gives a rough estimate of the shape characteristics of the desired implant and the implant's position in the coarse skull.

## 2.2 Defective Region Extraction

Notice that the first step provides an approximate position of the cranial defect along with the coarse profile of the desired implant at a resolution of $128 \times 128 \times 64$. In the second step, the coarse implant obtained in step 1 is upsampled back to the resolution of $512 \times 512 \times z$, and a bounding box is generated around the predicted implant with a certain margin around the edges of the coarse implant. The bounding box here gives an idea of the location and the estimated size of the defect. We relocate this bounding box back in the defective skull to extract some region around the defect. We refer to the region enclosed within the bounding box as our Region of Interest (RoI), which can be seen in the Fig. 2.

The defective region extraction is crucial because the pattern of the neighbouring voxels around the defect in the defective skull can help us estimate the part of the skull lost in the defect, and using that, the implant can be predicted more efficiently.

## 2.3 Implant Reconstruction

In the previous step, the RoI around the cranial defect is extracted through the bounding box obtained from the low-resolution implant.

We use another encoder-decoder network N2, for the reconstruction purpose. The RoI obtained after the defective region extraction is fed as input to the N2 network to predict the reconstructed RoI. The ground truth is the region enclosed within the bounding box when relocated in the complete skull corresponding to defective input.

Notice that reconstructing a small region has multiple advantages. Firstly, it speeds up the training process. Secondly, it helps get rid of the unwanted inconsistencies that would have occurred with direct implant generation. Finally, it also improves the accuracy of reconstruction when compared to performing the reconstruction over the entire skull.

Next, the fine high-resolution implant is obtained by subtracting the input RoI from the predicted output. This approach produces an accurate implant as the subtraction of the defective region from the restored region does not produce any inconsistencies around the edges.

The implant obtained after the subtraction process could still contain some islands floating around it. These islands are removed using connected components analysis by retaining only the largest connected component. Figure 3 illustrates the effect of performing the connected- component based post-processing on the resulting implant.

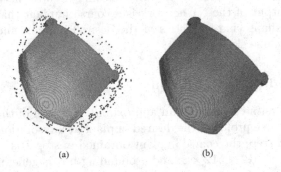

(a)                                          (b)

**Fig. 3.** The cranial implant (a) before post-processing and (b) after post-processing.

## 2.4   V-Net Architecture

V-Net is similar to U-Net [19], which is another famous deep learning architecture for image segmentation and has been extensively used by several proposed solutions in AutoImplant 2020. Despite their similarities, V-Net has some significant differences from U-Net. Firstly, the V-Net architecture uses 3D convolutions that learn volumetric information, rather than slice wise as in the case of the U-Net, which is a 2D architecture.

Secondly, in V-Net, there are skip connections present within the encoding and decoding blocks, concatenating the input of every block to its output feature

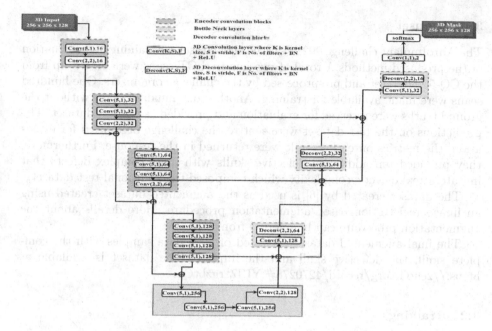

**Fig. 4.** Illustration of the V-Net architecture used in the N1 and N2 encoder-decoders of the proposed method.

map, which help in learning a residual function. The residual learning at every encoding and decoding block ensures better convergence in comparison to non-residual architectures such as U-Net as mentioned in [17]. Due to these features, in our proposed method, V-Net is chosen for both the encoder-decoder networks. Figure 4 illustrates the V-Net architecture we are using in our proposed method.

It consists of four encoder blocks, one bottleneck convolution block, and three decoding blocks followed by $(1 \times 1 \times 1)$ convolution and softmax activation. The encoder blocks consist of 3D convolution layers with kernel dimensions as $(5 \times 5 \times 5)$ and $(2 \times 2 \times 2)$ with a stride of 1 and 2, respectively. The decoder blocks consist $(5 \times 5 \times 5)$ 3D convolution layers with a stride 1, and $(2 \times 2 \times 2)$ 3D deconvolution layers with stride 2. The network consists of skip connections within every encoding and decoding block. The network also consists of skip connections from the encoder feature maps to each stage of the decoder layer.

# 3   Results

This section is organized as follows. Sect. 3.1 presents the details of the dataset. The details of training and hyper-parameters are presented in Sect. 3.2. Section 3.3 presents the evaluation results. An ablation study is presented in the next section, i.e. Sect. 3.4. Finally, the manufacturing process and the 3D printed design of the predicted implants are presented in Sect. 3.5.

## 3.1    Dataset

The AutoImplant challenge 2021 released the dataset for training and evaluation of the proposed methods.A total of two hundred CT scans were picked up from the CQ-500 dataset and pre-processed by the challenge organizers. One hundred scans were made available for training. Another one-hundred scans without the ground truths were reserved for evaluation and provided as the test dataset. The predictions on the test dataset were sent to the challenge organizers for evaluation, the metrics on each sample were returned in the response. Furthermore, they provided ten additional defective skulls with more complex defects that imitate a real defect's complexity which composed the additional test dataset.

The dataset created by [6] is used as the augmented dataset created using an image registration based augmentation procedure. More details about the augmentation procedure can be referred from [18].

The final augmented dataset consisted of 9908 data samples with the complete skull, the defective skull and the implant. The dataset is available at https://zenodo.org/record/4270278#.YUlZ_rgzbtQ.

## 3.2    Training

The training was accelerated with the help of an RTX 3000 GPU with N1 and N2 encoder-decoder being trained for 25,000 training steps each, and it approximately took two days and four days to train N1 and N2 encoder-decoder networks, respectively. The learning rate for the first model was 0.001, with a decay rate of 0.03. The training involved minimisation over the dice loss, which is obtained as:

$$\text{dice loss} = 1 - \text{DSC} \tag{1}$$

We used Adam as an optimizer and L1 regularization when training N1. We chose to use L1-regularization here because the predicted coarse implant is a sparse output compared to the defective skull as an input. Since our goal is to estimate the boundary of the implant, the first network N1 does not require smoothness constraint that is commonly ensured by L2-regularization. The second network N2 is trained for 25000 steps, and the best performing model is chosen. In N2, we used L2 regularization because the objective is to predict a smooth surface which is the reconstructed skull within the selected RoI.

## 3.3    Evaluations

The metrics used for evaluation are the Dice Similarity Coefficient (DSC), Border Dice Similarity Coefficient (BDSC), the Hausdorff Distance (HD), and the HD95. The DSC measures the extent of spatial overlap between two volumes. Let A and B represent the ground truth and the predicted implant, respectively. Thus, for volumes A and B, the DSC is given by:

$$\text{DSC} = 2 \times (A \cap B)/(A + B) \tag{2}$$

BDSC measures how accurately the predicted implant fits around the border of the defective skull by computing the DSC between the predicted implant and the ground truth only for the region close to the boundary of the defective skull.

The Hausdorff distance gives the maximum of the minimum distances between each voxel in the two volumes. For two volumes A and B, HD is given by:

$$HD = \max(\min(d(A, B))),    \text{(3)}$$

where $\min(d(A,B))$ is the set of mimimum distances between each voxel in volume A with other voxels in volume B. Finally, HD95 represents the 95 percentile of the HD. Table 1 presents the evaluation metrics for the two datasets. The dataset with scans 0–100 achieved a dice score of 0.93, border dice of 0.97 and HD95 of 1.57 mm, whereas by including the given additional ten scans for the dataset, our proposed model obtained a dice score of 0.9, border dice of 0.95 and HD95 of 2.02 mm. The box plots for the dataset of 110 scans is shown in Fig. 5.

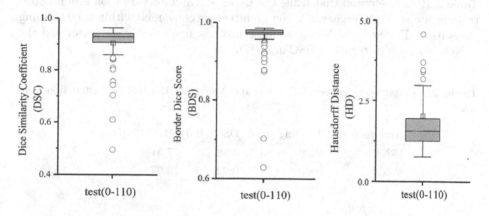

**Fig. 5.** The box plots of different metrics on the test and additional test datasets

**Table 1.** Metrics obtained on two test sets using the proposed method.

| Test (0–100) | | | Test (0–110) | | |
| --- | --- | --- | --- | --- | --- |
| DSC | BDSC | HD95 (mm) | DSC | BDSC | HD95 (mm) |
| 0.93 | 0.97 | 1.57 | 0.90 | 0.95 | 2.02 |

## 3.4 Ablation Study

We experimented with a number of different architectures such as the U-Net++ [22], which is a nested variant of U-Net [19] before finalizing our architectures for N1 and N2 encoder-decoders as the V-Net. The 3D U-Net++ architecture consists of many skip connections that propagate the information extracted in the initial layers of the encoder to the final layers of the decoder. Since U-Net has already been used extensively in AutoImplant 2020, we had the statistics on its performance for the direct implant generation and shape completion approaches. On the other hand, V-Net was also used previously in proposed methods for AutoImplant 2020 and gave good results for both the direct approach and shape completion approach.

Both the V-Net and U-Net++ are evaluated for the RoI reconstruction approach.

The U-Net++ used was an ensemble-3 variant for N1, and an ensemble-4 variant for N2 respectively. There were four encoding-decoding layers in N1 and five encoding-decoding layers in N2. Each encoding layer consisted of a 3D Convolution block with ReLU activation and batch normalization. The encoding decoding layers had high skip connections between them. The U-Net++ used in N2 had approximately 9 million training parameters.

The evaluation results obtained from both the networks are summarized in Table 2. It can be noted that while the U-Net++ architecture took around 8000 training steps to converge, the V-Net architecture converged within 5000 training steps itself. Further, the V-Net architecture has significantly outperformed the U-Net++, both in terms of DSC and HD.

**Table 2.** Comparison between U-Net++ and V-Net for the RoI reconstruction approach

| Architectures | Training steps | DSC (100) | HD (100)(mm) |
|---------------|----------------|-----------|--------------|
| U-Net++       | 8000           | 0.88      | 7.31         |
| V-Net         | 5000           | 0.92      | 3.97         |

## 3.5   Manufacturing Cranial Implant Through 3D Printing

Closing the cranial defect after the primary surgery usually takes a long time due to the range of standardized procedures involved, such as the implant design, manufacturing and sterilization. However, an "in-operating-room" design and manufacturing process is essential to conduct the secondary surgery for closing the cranial defect to avoid the functional and physical damages that would occur if the skull is left uncovered. The concern is also increased due to the risk of infections that might enter the brain, leading to fatalities. Also, the duration between the modelling and actual printing of the implant needs to be very less. The duration needs to be less to insure a good implant design even after the onset of preliminary healing [12]. This can be ensured only through in house production of cranial implants. To explore such practical aspects of the cranial implant design, we conducted experiments through 3D printing for generating the skull and the implant predicted by an earlier version of our current proposed model.

The defective skull, complete skull and the predicted cranial implant are converted into 3D models for the 3D printing process using the 3D Slicer software [7]. We conducted various experiments considering the material properties, orientation and temperature requirements for 3D printing. We selected a test case from the training set (implant corresponding to 001.nrrd) and printed the skull with cranial defect and its corresponding ground-truth implant for comparison using Thermoplastic Poly-Utherane (TPU) material as mentioned earlier. In Fig. 6 we can see multiple views of the 3D printed defective skull using TPU. The process used for 3D printing the defective skull was the fused deposition modelling [1] which is an additive manufacturing process suitable for plastic powders.

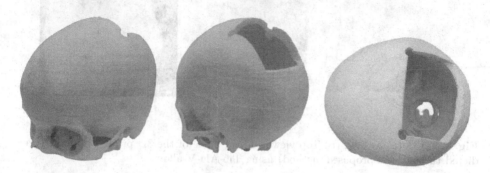

**Fig. 6.** Different views of the the defective skull 3D printed using TPU.

The material we used for generating the medical-grade implant is Ti6-Al4-V, which is the standard titanium-aluminium alloy used for medical prosthetics and implants. The process used for 3D printing the alloy-based implant was selective laser melting [10] which is a material efficient, additive manufacturing process suitable for metals and alloys.

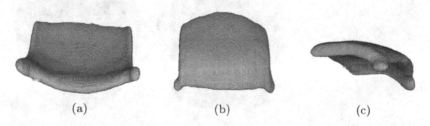

(a)                              (b)                              (c)

**Fig. 7.** Front view (180 °C flipped), top view and side view of the solid model of the cranial implant in STL format.

The material chosen should have the properties such as 'bio-compatibility-to avoid the chemical reactions with the brain tissues, 'diagnostic compatibility'

- that will not create artefacts with CT or MRI imaging, 'implantability' - to
have smaller size or shape adjustments by neurosurgeons and 'thermally stable'-
to sustain to high or low temperatures. Figure 7 illustrates the STL format of
the generated implant from the proposed method in multiple views. The most
material-efficient orientation for printing was 180 °C. (refer to the first image in
Fig. 7). Figure 8(a) shows the implant with the support structures upon which
it is 3D printed, whereas Fig. 8(b) shows the bottom view of the implant after
removing the supporting structures.

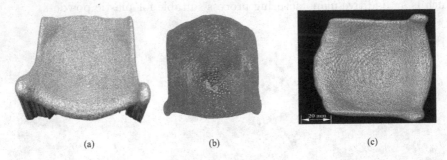

(a)                         (b)                         (c)

**Fig. 8.** (a) Bottom view, (b) Top view, and (c) Scale of the 3D printed implant (predicted through the proposed method) using Ti6-Al4-V alloy.

Finally, Fig. 9(a) shows the ground truth. Figure 9(b) and (c) show the fit
of the implant predicted using the proposed method. While there are gaps still
visible at the edges of the implant, overall, it fits the defective cranium well in
the defective region.

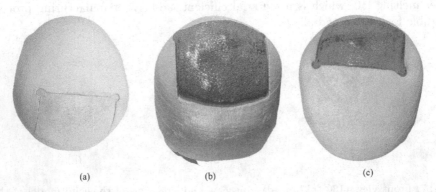

(a)                         (b)                         (c)

**Fig. 9.** (a) The complete skull (ground truth) using TPU material and (b), (c) the top
views of defective skull after placing the Ti6-Al4-V based implant on the defect.

# 4  Conclusions and Discussions

In this paper, we propose an efficient two-step approach that involves localization of the defective region followed by reconstruction of the implant. The proposed method is similar to the baseline approach because both methods use a two-step approach for defect extraction and reconstruction. However, the proposed method differs from [13] in the following ways: Firstly, the existing method performs a direct implant generation, whereas the proposed method reconstructs the region of interest. Secondly, we proposed using V-Net architecture for both stages instead of a simple encoder-decoder network. Using V-Net in the proposed method produced the cranial implants with high accuracy compared to U-Net++. To the best of our knowledge, this is the first implant design performed through skull reconstruction in the region of interest, which has drastically reduced the computational complexity. The reduction of the prediction region also enabled efficient training and the faster convergence of deep learning models. In addition, we 3D printed the cranial implant predicted by our model using bio-compatible material, a titanium-aluminium alloy (Ti6-Al4-V), to investigate the practical feasibility of the automated designs. The proposed model has resulted in an average dice similarity score of 0.90 and a 95 percentile Hausdorff distance of 2.02mm. In future work, we plan to take into account the practical aspects involved during the surgery.

# References

1. Ahn, S.H., Montero, M., Odell, D., Roundy, S., Wright, P.K.: Anisotropic material properties of fused deposition modeling abs. Rap. Prototyp. J. **8**, 248–257 (2002)
2. Bayat, A., Shit, S., Kilian, A., Liechtenstein, J.T., Kirschke, J.S., Menze, B.H.: Cranial implant prediction using low-resolution 3D shape completion and high-resolution 2D refinement. In: Cranial Implant Design Challenge. pp. 77–84. Springer (2020)
3. von Campe, G., Pistracher, K.: Patient specific implants (PSI). In: Li, J., Egger, J. (eds.) AutoImplant 2020. LNCS, vol. 12439, pp. 1–9. Springer, Cham (2020). https://doi.org/10.1007/978-3-030-64327-0_1
4. Casamitjana, A., Catà, M., Sánchez, I., Combalia, M., Vilaplana, V.: Cascaded V-Net using ROI masks for brain tumor segmentation. In: Crimi, A., Bakas, S., Kuijf, H., Menze, B., Reyes, M. (eds.) BrainLes 2017. LNCS, vol. 10670, pp. 381–391. Springer, Cham (2018). https://doi.org/10.1007/978-3-319-75238-9_33
5. Eder, M., Li, J., Egger, J.: Learning volumetric shape super-resolution for cranial implant design. In: Cranial Implant Design Challenge. pp. 104–113. Springer, Cham (2020)
6. Ellis, D.G., Aizenberg, M.R.: Deep learning using augmentation via registration: 1st place solution to the autoimplant 2020 challenge. In: Cranial Implant Design Challenge. pp. 47–55. Springer (2020)
7. Fedorov, A., Beichel, R., Kalpathy-Cramer, J., Finet, J., Fillion-Robin, J.C., Pujol, S., Bauer, C., Jennings, D., Fennessy, F., Sonka, M., et al.: 3D slicer as an image computing platform for the quantitative imaging network. Mag. Resonan. Imag. **30**(9), 1323–1341 (2012)

8. Jin, Y., Li, J., Egger, J.: High-resolution cranial implant prediction via patch-wise training. In: Cranial Implant Design Challenge. pp. 94–103. Springer (2020)
9. Kodym, O., Španěl, M., Herout, A.: Cranial defect reconstruction using cascaded cnn with alignment. In: Cranial Implant Design Challenge. pp. 56–64. Springer (2020)
10. Kruth, J.P., Froyen, L., Van Vaerenbergh, J., Mercelis, P., Rombouts, M., Lauwers, B.: Selective laser melting of iron-based powder. J. Mater. Process. Technol. **149**(1–3), 616–622 (2004)
11. Lei, Y., Tian, S., He, X., Wang, T., Wang, B., Patel, P., Jani, A.B., Mao, H., Curran, W.J., Liu, T., et al.: Ultrasound prostate segmentation based on multidirectional deeply supervised v-net. Med. Phys. **46**(7), 3194–3206 (2019)
12. Li, J., Egger, J.: Towards the Automatization of Cranial Implant Design in Cranioplasty. Springer, Cham (2020). https://doi.org/10.1007/978-3-030-64327-0
13. Li, J., Pepe, A., Gsaxner, C., Campe, G., Egger, J.: A baseline approach for AutoImplant: the MICCAI 2020 cranial implant design challenge. In: Syeda-Mahmood, T., Drechsler, K., Greenspan, H., Madabhushi, A., Karargyris, A., Linguraru, M.G., Oyarzun Laura, C., Shekhar, R., Wesarg, S., González Ballester, M.Á., Erdt, M. (eds.) CLIP/ML-CDS -2020. LNCS, vol. 12445, pp. 75–84. Springer, Cham (2020). https://doi.org/10.1007/978-3-030-60946-7_8
14. Li, J., et al.: Autoimplant 2020-first miccai challenge on automatic cranial implant design. IEEE Trans. Med. Imag. **40**(9), 2329–2342 (2021). https://doi.org/10.1109/TMI.2021.3077047
15. Mainprize, J.G., Fishman, Z., Hardisty, M.R.: Shape completion by U-Net: an approach to the AutoImplant MICCAI cranial implant design challenge. In: Li, J., Egger, J. (eds.) AutoImplant 2020. LNCS, vol. 12439, pp. 65–76. Springer, Cham (2020). https://doi.org/10.1007/978-3-030-64327-0_8
16. Matzkin, F., Newcombe, V., Glocker, B., Ferrante, E.: Cranial implant design via virtual craniectomy with shape priors. In: Cranial Implant Design Challenge, pp. 37–46. Springer, Cham (2020)
17. Milletari, F., Navab, N., Ahmadi, S.A.: V-net: Fully convolutional neural networks for volumetric medical image segmentation. In: 2016 Fourth International Conference on 3D Vision (3DV), pp. 565–571. IEEE (2016)
18. Nalepa, J., et al.: Data augmentation via image registration. In: 2019 IEEE International Conference on Image Processing (ICIP), pp. 4250–4254. IEEE (2019)
19. Ronneberger, O., Fischer, P., Brox, T.: U-Net: convolutional networks for biomedical image segmentation. In: Navab, N., Hornegger, J., Wells, W.M., Frangi, A.F. (eds.) MICCAI 2015. LNCS, vol. 9351, pp. 234–241. Springer, Cham (2015). https://doi.org/10.1007/978-3-319-24574-4_28
20. Shi, H., Chen, X.: Cranial implant design through multiaxial slice inpainting using deep learning. In: Li, J., Egger, J. (eds.) AutoImplant 2020. LNCS, vol. 12439, pp. 28–36. Springer, Cham (2020). https://doi.org/10.1007/978-3-030-64327-0_4
21. Wang, B., Liu, Z., Li, Y., Xiao, X., Zhang, R., Cao, Y., Cui, L., Zhang, P.: Cranial implant design using a deep learning method with anatomical regularization. In: Li, J., Egger, J. (eds.) AutoImplant 2020. LNCS, vol. 12439, pp. 85–93. Springer, Cham (2020). https://doi.org/10.1007/978-3-030-64327-0_10
22. Zhou, Z., Rahman Siddiquee, M.M., Tajbakhsh, N., Liang, J., et al.: UNet++: a nested U-Net architecture for medical image segmentation. In: Stoyanov, D. (ed.) DLMIA/ML-CDS -2018. LNCS, vol. 11045, pp. 3–11. Springer, Cham (2018). https://doi.org/10.1007/978-3-030-00889-5_1

# Author Index

Printed in the United States
by Baker & Taylor Publisher Services

Printed in the United States
by Baker & Taylor Publisher Services